MW01064908

Dirty Faith is a straight-up, practical guide for young people who are ready to step beyond Bible study to reach hurting people with the love of God. For the sake of those who need you, read it — now!"

BART CAMPOLO, president, Mission Year

"The youth of today are looking for true, authentic Christ-followers who have understood the grace of Jesus and changed the way they live their lives. Audio Adrenaline and Mark Matlock have slam-dunked with clarity what it really looks like to serve Jesus Christ in the 21st century, and they have done it in plain English that you don't need a seminary degree to understand. We are without excuse. Let's live for Him!"

ROY PETERSON, executive director, The Seed Company,
a ministry of Wycliffe Bible Translators

"Never have I seen anything like Christian students today. They never have been interested in religion, but they're head-over-heels in love with Jesus. Far beyond sentimentality, they are ready to lock arms with the Master in changing the world. Dirty Faith *will be their field manual, providing concrete ways to express what is burning inside of them. Audio Adrenaline and Mark Matlock have just nailed the heart and soul of this new generation."*

DR. RICHARD ROSS, professor of student ministry,
Southwestern Baptist Theological Seminary, Fort Worth, Texas;
spokesperson, True Love Waits Campaign

*"*Dirty Faith *is the real deal! Once you read it, you'll want to get out there and experience Christ working all around you in the real world, where it's dirty. Audio Adrenaline and Mark Matlock have captured a timely truth on these pages that the church is desperately in need of and given practical solutions that will inspire, inform, and equip you to become the hands and feet of our Lord."*

FRED LYNCH, urban ministry coordinator,
Josh McDowell Ministries; author of *The Epic*

Go Ahead:

TH1NK: *about God*

about life

about others

Faith isn't just an act; it's something you live — something huge and sometimes unimaginable. By getting into the real issues in your life, TH1NK books open opportunities to talk honestly about your faith, your relationship with God and others, as well as all the things life throws at you.

Don't let other people th1nk for you . . .

TH1NK for yourself.

AUDIO ADRENALINE

WITH MARK MATLOCK

DIRTY FAITH

BECOMING THE HANDS AND FEET OF JESUS

Navpress
P.O. Box 35001
Colorado Springs, Colorado 80935

The Navigators is an international Christian organization. Our mission is to reach, disciple, and equip people to know Christ and to make Him known through successive generations. We envision multitudes of diverse people in the United States and every other nation who have a passionate love for Christ, live a lifestyle of sharing Christ's love, and multiply spiritual laborers among those without Christ.

NavPress is the publishing ministry of The Navigators. NavPress publications help believers learn biblical truth and apply what they learn to their lives and ministries. Our mission is to stimulate spiritual formation among our readers.

ISBN 1-57683-565-0

Cover design by The Office of Bill Chiaravalle, www.officeofbc.com, Benjamin Kinzer
Cover photo by The Office of Bill Chiaravalle, Benjamin Kinzer
Creative Team: Jay Howver, Liz Heaney, Cara Iverson, Glynese Northam

Song lyrics at chapter starts are from Audio Adrenaline's song "Hands and Feet."
"Hands and Feet" words and music by Mark Stuart, Bob Herdman, Will McGinniss, Tyler Burkum, and Charlie Peacock. © 1999 Up In The Mix Music/Andi Beat Goes On Music (BMI)/Flicker USA Publishing (BMI) Administered by EMI Christian Music Publishing. All Rights Reserved.
"Dirty" words and music by Mark Stuart, Will McGinniss, Bob Herdman, Tyler Burkum and Ben Cissell. © 2002 Up In The Mix Music/Flicker USA Publishing (BMI)Administered by EMI Christian Music Publishing. All Rights Reserved.

Some of the anecdotal illustrations in this book are true to life and are included with the permission of the persons involved. All other illustrations are composites of real situations, and any resemblance to people living or dead is coincidental.

Unless otherwise identified, all Scripture quotations in this publication are taken from the *New King James Version* (NKJV). Copyright © 1982 by Thomas Nelson, Inc. Used by permission. All rights reserved. Other versions used include: the HOLY BIBLE: NEW INTERNATIONAL VERSION® (NIV®), copyright © 1973, 1978, 1984 by International Bible Society, used by permission of Zondervan Publishing House, all rights reserved; and *THE MESSAGE* (MSG), copyright © 1993, 1994, 1995, 1996, 2000, 2001, 2002, used by permission of NavPress Publishing Group.

Dirty faith : becoming the hands and feet of Jesus / Audio Adrenaline
with Mark Matlock.
    p. cm.
  ISBN 1-57683-565-0 (pbk.)
  1. Youth--Religious life. 2. Christian life. I. Matlock, Mark. II.
Audio Adrenaline (Musical group)
  BV4531.3.D57 2003
  248.8'3--dc22

                       2003017220

Printed in Canada

1 2 3 4 5 6 7 8 9 10 / 07 06 05 04 03

This book is dedicated to the members of Wycliffe Bible Translators, who dirty their hands and feet every day to bring the Word of God to people who have never heard it so they might have faith and get dirty too.

CONTENTS

ACKNOWLEDGMENTS

"Plans fail for lack of counsel," King Solomon wrote in Proverbs, and the same is true when assembling a book like this: Counsel is important. We'd like to thank Chris Lyon for his tremendous effort in making this book happen and also Natalie Newberry and Rachel Lipps for pre-reading the manuscript and giving us their expert student opinions.

INTRODUCTION

Tired of being clean, sick of being proper
I wanna live among the beggars and dig out in the dirt
Step outside the walls we built to protect us
Don't be afraid to get some mud on your face
— FROM "DIRTY" ON AUDIO ADRENALINE'S *WORLDWIDE* CD

For too long, many Christians have defined this path we're on by what we *don't* do. Especially for students, being a Christian has meant that we don't party; we don't have sex; we don't drink or smoke or do drugs. Too many leaders left us with the idea that standing out from the world meant staying home and *not* doing stuff. They seemed to care more about keeping us clean and sober than they did about sending us out there to turn the world upside down.

Now hold on. Nobody's saying we should give up living clean lives. That's definitely *part* of what God tells us to do. Paul wrote that we must "behave decently" (Romans 13:13, NIV) by steering away from sexual immorality and drunkenness. One portion of our job is to lead such clean lives that the world has nothing to accuse us of (see 1 Peter 2:12).

But if we just stop at clean living and don't *do* anything else, we're not really living. We're not really loving people. We just turn into religious items in a display case: "Look at how clean these Christians are! They never move at all! The world never touches them! They're spotless!"

Nope. God wants us to climb down off the shelf and get to work. Being a Christian does mean being clean. But it also means taking action, getting involved, being used to getting God's work done. In other words, it's time for God's people to get dirty.

Guess what? Getting dirty by going to work for God is much harder than staying clean by not having sex before you're married and not drinking. It's one thing to say "no thanks" to drugs. That just makes sense, doesn't it? It doesn't take huge faith in God to say "no." The big faith is needed when it's time to say "yes." Saying "yes" to God is what grows Christian babies into Christian men, women, and heroes.

That's right—heroes. Ever heard of the Hall of Faith in Hebrews 11? It's a much more impressive collection of heroes than the Justice League. It's a collection of real people living in the hard world who found the courage to say "yes" to God when He told them to do some unbelievable things. These people proved their faith by doing something about it: They got down and got dirty for God.

What did they do? Well, Noah built that giant boat with no water in sight just because God told him to. He was already known in the neighborhood as a guy who lived a pretty clean life. But this pushed his reputation over the edge to becoming "the guy who believed God enough to do something crazy." And it saved him and his family from the flood (see Genesis 7-8; Hebrews 11:7).

Abraham did all kinds of crazy-sounding stuff just because God said so. He packed up everything he had and moved to the middle of nowhere. He believed God could give him and his wife a kid even though they were way too old. And he was willing to kill that son when God said to, believing God could just bring him right back to life (see Genesis 12:1-5).

Were these guys perfect believers? Not at all. How about all the other heroes of Hebrews 11? How about Moses and Rahab and Joshua and Gideon and Samson? Not even close. They all made huge human mistakes, like committing adultery and lying and getting drunk and disobeying God. So why are they heroes? Because they believed God and took a risk by doing what He told them. They weren't perfect, but they were willing to get dirty.

Do you believe that God tells the truth? If you're a Christian — if you've trusted in Jesus for salvation and heaven and a relationship with the Father — you believed God enough to take that first step. How about the next step? Do you still believe Him?

The very first verse in Hebrews 11 defines exactly what faith is: "Being sure of what we hope for and certain of what we do not see." Obeying God by getting involved doesn't mean waiting until we can see with our own eyes exactly why it makes perfect sense. It means trusting God's heart and His power and His goodness. It means believing that if He said it, it's true. It means getting dirty because He's trustworthy.

Flash-forward to the first verse of Hebrews 12. We've got all these heroes of the faith as our examples, right? So what should we do about it? The writer tells us it's like a race, and it's our turn to run. Every time we believe God and love someone who is hurting or help someone in need or tell another about Jesus, we take the next step on "the course marked out for us."

Every time we ignore God or let our fear keep us from doing the hard things He asks us to do, we stop moving. We stop running. We take ourselves out of the race. Too many of us have gotten comfortable sitting right in the middle of the track with a bag of chips in one hand and a remote control in the other. We're tired of the race. We know we're going to heaven, and we don't really want to get our hands dirty.

Hebrews 12 tells us that the answer to our apathy is one man: Jesus. He ran the race. He gives us the power to keep going. By keeping our eyes on Him, we can become His hands and feet on earth. Yep, we're going to get dirty just like He did. But He'll give us the strength to keep going (see verse 3).

This book is for people who are ready to be Jesus on earth. It's for people who want to stop being comfortable and cozy and instead get out there and get to work. It's for people who want to know how to roll up their sleeves and do more than just *not* do bad stuff. This book is for people who are ready to get dirty. Are *you* ready?

CHAPTER ONE

JESUS WHO?

An image flashed across my TV screen
Another broken heart comes into view
I saw the pain and I turned my back
Why can't I do the things I want to?

It was one of those reality shows. The girl had just found out she was pregnant. She didn't want to be pregnant. She was young. She thought she should be going to college, starting a career, doing *something* with her life. A baby right now would ruin everything. And the guy she had had sex with wasn't even close to daddy material. She decided she would have an abortion.

The pain in her eyes spoke louder than her words. She tried to sound casual: "It's my right. The baby isn't even a baby yet. Lots of women do it." But her eyes gave her away: "I'm not sure if this is right. I need help. How can this be happening to me?"

We kept seeing those eyes even after the TV was turned off. We kept talking about this and thinking, *Someone has to be there for her. Where are the Jesus-followers in her life? Someone should have said, "The Father still loves you — even though you had sex before marriage, even though you're thinking about abortion, even though you haven't talked to Him. He can take care of you and your baby. We'll be here. We'll help you."*

Where were Jesus' feet to walk with her through the pain of the decision? Where were Jesus' hands to hold hers and his ears to listen to her fears and her anger?

Then we caught our eyes in a mirror. Who knows us as Jesus' hands? How are we being Jesus' feet and eyes and mouth to the people in the world? What are we doing to get our faith dirty? What we mean is: How are we, just like Jesus, going to get into the lives of real people exactly where they live, roll up our sleeves, and meet their needs?

WWJD?: JUST A FAD?

A few years ago, someone brought up an old question in a new way: "What would Jesus do?" Based on the famous book *In His Steps*, by Charles Sheldon, "WWJD?" became a huge hit. Everywhere you went, you saw "WWJD?" on T-shirts and bracelets and bumper stickers and necklaces. There were "WWJD?" board games and cereals and websites and jackets. You couldn't listen to Christian radio or go to youth group or walk into a Christian bookstore without seeing or hearing "WWJD?"

Students, especially, got caught up in the idea of basing their everyday decisions on figuring out what Jesus would do if He were in their shoes. They wanted being a Christian to be something that really mattered, not just a place they went on Sundays. They wanted to reach out to the world with Jesus' love. In short, they wanted to be Jesus' hands and feet right here on earth. Wearing that bracelet was a way of saying, "I want to put my beliefs into *action*."

Eventually, like all fads, wearing the "WWJD?" message on your wrist or your chest or around your neck died off. It went out of fashion. It became "last year's style." People quietly put their bracelets away and left the T-shirts in the drawer. And that was fine. Jesus didn't call us to *wear* a message — He called us to live one.

Unfortunately, trying to live like Jesus also went out of style for many people. It just got too hard and confusing. Many of us realized that wearing that message didn't change us at all. It just made us feel bad when we lived exactly like Jesus never would.

Another problem was that lots of people didn't know how to answer the question. What *would* Jesus do? Who knows? One clever Bible study company came out with shoestring bracelets that said, "HDYKWJWDIYDKWHD?" (It was a *long* shoestring.) Translation: "How do you know what Jesus would do if you don't know what He did?" You can't be Jesus' hands and feet in your part of the world if you don't know what Jesus did with *His* hands and feet when He was on earth. You've got to get to know the Man before you can live like Him.

In this chapter of our book, we want to talk a little bit about who Jesus was (and is!). Hold on. Anytime you're learning about Jesus, you've got to be ready for God to turn your world upside down. This was no ordinary guy.

HANDS AND FEET IN ACTION

THE MISSION YEAR FILES

NOTE: MISSION YEAR IS AN ORGANIZATION THAT ENCOURAGES STUDENTS TO MOVE INTO THE INNER CITY FOR ONE YEAR IN ORDER TO BE JESUS' HANDS AND FEET AS NEIGHBORS TO THE POOR AND THE BROKEN. SEE PAGE 143 TO FIND OUT MORE ABOUT MISSION YEAR.

With his black toga, sandals, greasy beard, and white doily head-
band, Ray was quite a sight in the courtyard of the Presbyterian
church. A conference had just let out, and everyone kept his or her
distance. I watched Ray roll his eyes after one bold conference mem-
ber quickly set a packaged sandwich from lunch on the bench beside
him, said "God bless you," and quickly walked away.

Moments later, Ray turned his attention toward me and started
mumbling angry comments. With nothing to do until my ride came,
I sat down and listened to him for a while. Between Ray's drug-
induced blackouts and spurts of vulgarity, I caught passionate
flashes of wisdom and sincere pain.

Well into an hour of the best conversation you could hope for
under the circumstances, something began to break through — some-
thing that had been ignored for too many months of holding
Styrofoam cups along the university sidewalks. Ray's eyes bored
into mine, pleading me not to look away. He expressed his own
wretchedness and spoke of Jesus. He gripped my hand, and tears
came to my eyes, washing away my self-righteous skepticism.

At one point, Ray set down his tall malt liquor to hold my
shoulders and say, "This is the love of Christ." Then he hugged me
firmly in the middle of the now-empty courtyard, and I totally
understood. I've never felt so used of God in touching another
person's life.

— CASS, MISSION YEAR VOLUNTEER

SEVEN QUESTIONS

Before we get started, try the following quiz to find out how much you know about Jesus' life:

1. How long has Jesus been around?
   a. Since the 1960s
   b. For about two thousand years
   c. Since the beginning of time
   d. Since before time began

2. How are Jesus and God the Father related?
   a. Jesus is the Son of God the Father.
   b. Jesus and the Father are the same person.
   c. Jesus and the Father are both part of the Trinity.
   d. All of the above.

3. How long had Joseph and Mary been married when Jesus was born?
   a. Ten years.
   b. Five years.
   c. A few weeks.
   d. They weren't married yet.

4. What race was Jesus in His humanity?
   a. English
   b. Arab
   c. Jewish
   d. Mixed race

5. How many times did Jesus sin?
   a. He never sinned.
   b. He almost never sinned.

c. Who knows if He sinned or not?

d. He sinned as much as anyone, but He was a good person.

6. **How many people saw Jesus after He had died and come back to life?**

a. Nobody saw Him.

b. Only His disciples saw Him.

c. Over five hundred people saw Him.

d. Over fifty thousand people saw Him.

7. **What reason did Jesus give for coming to earth?**

a. To look for the lost

b. To give His life to pay for other people's sin

c. To do what His Father wanted

d. All of the above

e. To rule the planet

How'd you do? Read on to find the answers to each of these questions about Jesus.

1.   ALWAYS   AROUND

Unlike you and me, Jesus didn't just come into existence on the day He was conceived. John 1 tells us that Jesus was "in the beginning" with God the Father. That means Jesus existed before time began.

Why does that matter? Because it's part of who Jesus is — He's eternal. The word *eternal* literally means "outside of time." Other than the thirty-three years or so He spent on our planet, Jesus isn't limited by hours and days and weeks — He's completely free!

His existence before creation also means He was involved in creating everything that has ever existed — including you! John 1:3 says that nothing created was made without Jesus. And David, the king of Israel, wrote that the Lord "formed my inward parts" (Psalm 139:13).

How awesome it is to know that the same Jesus who healed the sick and gave comfort with His hands actually made you. Who could know you better than your creator?

2. COMPLETELY GOD

This is a mind-bender, but it's huge in figuring out who Jesus is. Not only is He God's Son, but He's also completely God (as is the Holy Spirit). John, again, says that Jesus was with God and He *was* God (see John 1:1). It's hard to imagine how both those things could be true, but they are.

Jesus wasn't just a human man with God inside Him. He wasn't half God and half man. Instead, He was all God and all man. He was 100 percent of both. Before Jesus, nobody had ever seen God. God's holiness would kill them. But by coming to earth in a human body, Jesus allowed us to see God in action (see John 1:18).

In the 1990s, a singer named Joan Osborne had a hit song that asked the question, "What if God was one of us?" But the question really isn't on target. He *was* one of us. God was *here*, and He proved He loved us by dying for us.

3. NO EARTHLY DAD

On the night Jesus was born, Mary and Joseph still hadn't wed. Luke 2:5 calls Mary Joseph's "betrothed wife." *Betrothed* means "promised" or engaged. They weren't yet married and they hadn't yet had sex (see Matthew 1:25).

Why would God set things up like that? Why wouldn't He have arranged things so Jesus was born into the earthly family of a married couple with a great reputation? Didn't God realize people would assume Joseph had gotten Mary pregnant before he married her? Didn't God realize what that would do to Jesus' reputation?

God knew. But God doesn't care as much about reputation as He does about the truth. And the truth was that Joseph was not Jesus' birth dad — God was. In a miraculous way we don't fully get, God caused Mary to become pregnant without her ever having had sex (see Luke 1:34-35).

4. A JEWISH MAN

To really get Jesus, you have to understand that He was born a Jewish man in a Jewish culture. Everything about Jesus' life and times was Jewish. He was even descended directly from King David (see Matthew 1). You don't get more Jewish than that!

Why does it matter? It means Jesus understood the Old Testament ways inside and out. All those stories about the Israelites in Egypt and the desert and the time of the kings were stories about Jesus' people. He lived in a world of animal sacrifices and worshiping God at the temple. His family lived according to the Old Testament Law. They obeyed the rules about what and when to eat, work, and celebrate and how to pay for their sin. And they listened to Jewish Pharisees and other religious leaders teach about God.

Jesus lived in a country that had been conquered and occupied by another nation. At the time Jesus lived, the Romans ruled the world — including Israel. Rome set up governors to rule over all the conquered nations. So Jesus' country was being run by a foreign army. And sometimes those Roman soldiers could be cruel, especially if they thought a group of Israelites threatened their power.

5. TOTALLY SIN FREE

No other human being has ever done what Jesus did from the day of His birth—live a lifetime without sinning. A good definition of sin is "doing something my way instead of God's." Jesus was 100 percent obedient to His Father His whole life.

"Yeah," some people say, "but He was God. I could be sinless too if I were God." You really think so? If you had all the power in the universe, do you really think you could overcome the temptation to do things your own way even once? Satan was created without sin and he had way less power than Jesus. He couldn't handle it.

In fact, when we realize that Jesus was God in a fully human body, it's even more incredible that He never sinned. He had all the same physical desires and emotions any healthy man has. He wanted things. And He could have had anything He wanted. Still, He never sinned.

Oh, He had the chance. Satan made sure of that. Jesus spent forty days fasting and praying. He was hungry (see Matthew 4:2). That's when Satan showed up and gave Jesus three chances to do it Satan's way instead of God's way. Satan offered Jesus food, glory, and power. Jesus used Scripture to reject all three (see Matthew 4:1-11).

Okay, okay. So He never sinned. Cool. So what? Well, if Jesus had sinned, we'd be toast. The only reason He was qualified to die for our sins is because He didn't have any of His own to pay for. That makes it a very big deal.

6. HALF A THOUSAND

Even in Paul's day, some people wanted to be "sophisticated, educated" Christians who learned a lot from Jesus but didn't really believe
in all that resurrection stuff. They saw Jesus' life and death as a helpful way of looking at the world, not as reality. Paul said they were
missing the whole point – and the hard facts.

So, what evidence did Paul give that Jesus lived again after He
died? Eyewitness testimony. And not just from the guys who lived
with Jesus during His time here. Paul wrote that Jesus was seen alive
postmortem by over five hundred people at once (see 1 Corinthians
15:6). The disciples also saw Him (see John 20:26-31). Paul had an
incredible encounter with Jesus (see Acts 9:1-19). Jesus lives.

7. MISSION ACCOMPLISHED

Jesus came to this planet with a specific mission. It's not what we
might have planned for a visit from the Son of God. It's not what
God's people, the Jews, had in mind for the Messiah, either.

The Israelites *were* expecting a Messiah. They had read prophecies in the Scriptures about a conquering Savior who would give them
victory over their enemies once and for all. They were ready for this
chosen one to lead them to great peace and freedom and prosperity.

The problem was that they hadn't put that together with other
prophecies (such as Isaiah 53) that talked about a Messiah suffering
to save them. Jesus came to fulfill those prophecies. The conquering
and kingdom building would come later. So why was He here if not
to kick the Romans out of Jerusalem and become the best king ever?

Mission 1. Jesus: "For the Son of Man has come to seek and to save that which was lost" (Luke 19:10).

Instead of a search-and-destroy mission, Jesus came on a search-and-rescue mission. He brought an offer to all of us lost ones to be found forever in heaven with God. He came to save us.

Mission 2. Jesus: "For I have come down from heaven, not to do My own will, but the will of Him who sent Me" (John 6:38).

Jesus wasn't running His own show. He wasn't carrying out His own plans. He was obeying His Father. God's will was the only motivation in Jesus' life. He came, lived, taught, healed, died, and rose again — all because that's what the Father wanted Him to do. He came to obey His Father.

HANDS AND FEET IN ACTION

THE MISSION YEAR FILES

The last swim class of the day had been over for about half an hour. Bill, a recently hired lifeguard at the YMCA where I teach swimming, was sitting on the steps out front, waiting for his ride. I had time to kill. I thought, Should I go and chat with Bill, or should I finish the rest of my half-eaten peanut butter sandwich? I opted for Bill.

So there we were — me, wearing shorts and my favorite Hawaiian Island Creation T-shirt, and Bill in his baggy jeans, baggy shirt, and Raiders cap, looking really tough and intimidating. We'd talked a few times, but we'd never had a real conversation. I made the first move.

Me: "How's it?"

Bill: "'Sup."

We chatted some more, and then he brought up Mission Year as a topic. So I told him what Mission Year was all about.

Bill: "Oh, so this Mission Year, it's like a Jesus thing or something?"

Me: "Yeah, totally."

A little smirk grew across my face. Bill's ears perked; he had a curious look on his face. This conversation was starting to come to life. But Bill was still confused.

Bill: "So, you moved from warm, sunny Hawaii to the ghetto. You're not getting paid. All you eat for lunch is peanut butter and jelly sandwiches and water every day. And you're actually enjoying teaching these kids how to swim . . . for free?"

Me: "Yep."

I felt excitement, joy, and adrenaline. A relationship with Bill had just sparked. I wanted to tackle him and give him a giant hug for seeing why I was here. I almost jumped six feet in the air. It was hard to restrain myself. Bill was on to me, though. He raised his eyebrows.

Bill: "Wha . . . wha . . . why?"

There it was. My window of opportunity. I replied without thinking twice.

Me: "It's a Jesus thing."

Bill's facial expression changed. He shrugged his shoulders and gave me a smirk of approval.

Bill: "Jesus thing, huh? That's cool. I appreciate what you're doing here, bro."

Just then, Bill's ride pulled up. We shook hands and gave each other a half hug. A relationship was born and the seeds of Christ were planted. The next day, Bill surprised me and brought me a Pepsi to go along with my peanut butter and jelly sandwich. We talked again — not as strangers, but as friends.

— ANDREW, MISSION YEAR VOLUNTEER

Mission 3. Jesus: "The Son of Man did not come to be served, but to serve, and to give His life as a ransom for many" (Matthew 20:28).

We don't really understand the idea of a servant these days. Up until a few hundred years ago, whole groups of people worked as servants for others. A rich guy might have a dozen or so servants working in his house. One would do his cooking, one would clean, one would make the bed, one would take care of the garden, and all of them would do whatever the master told them to.

A servant's whole job was just to make the master happy. Today, we think of that as a lowly position, but it used to be an honorable thing to serve another person well.

Still, for Jesus to say His mission was to serve mere human beings doesn't add up. He is the Son of God. He made us. He should be giving the orders. But it's right there in red letters. Jesus came to serve people—to meet their needs and do the dirty work they can't do for themselves.

Ultimately, He served us all by dying to pay for our sins. We were hostages to death. Death was going to kill us all off, one by one forever, unless someone paid the ransom. Jesus did that. As the only sinless one, He served us by paying for our sin with His own life. Now death can't hold us. We've got an eternal life waiting for us in heaven.

So Jesus came to look for and save the lost ones, to obey His Father, and to serve mere, sinful humans by dying for us. Is that the way you think of Jesus?

HANDS AND FEET

So what does that mean for us, right now, today? How should we live if we're going to be Jesus' hands and feet on earth?

First, we're going to go looking for people who don't know Jesus. Because we all used to be lost in our sin, we should know what these people look like. They're the searching, hurting ones. They want something to believe in that will give their lives meaning and purpose, but they're afraid to trust too much in any one thing. They need to find Jesus, but they don't know it yet.

Unfortunately, we won't find these people by sitting on our couches watching the tube. Oh, we'll see a lot of them, but we won't meet them. To look for the lost, we're going to have to go outside and get to know them. We're going to have to make friends with them as Jesus did. Then, when they turn a corner and realize how lost they are, we'll be there to point them to Him (see 1 Peter 3:15).

Next, to live as Jesus' hands and feet, we're going to have to make up our minds every day that our reason for living is to do what God wants (instead of what we want). Like Jesus, we're going to have to learn to say, "Not my will but Yours be done, Father" (see Luke 22:42).

Jesus never used His hands and feet to do anything the Father didn't want done. As His servants on earth today, we've got to give up our desire to live for ourselves. Jesus' hands and feet always do God's will.

Finally, to follow in His steps, we've got to serve each other until we die. Sounds like fun, huh? Doesn't make for a very good bumper sticker. But that's what Jesus used His hands and feet for. He served others. He explained hard ideas to simple people. He spent days healing those who hurt. And He eventually served us so hard that blood and water ran out of His side and He died.

We've been given gifts we can use to serve each other: helping, encouraging, teaching, and a lot of others. (Read 1 Corinthians 12 to see how Paul talks about gifts.) To be Jesus' hands and feet, we've got to turn those words into actions and let the world see His hands and feet. People who spend their lives serving start looking more and more like Jesus.

Still want to be Jesus' hands and feet? Nothing in your life will ever matter more. It's not the easy road, but it's the only one worth traveling. Keep reading — you'll see how you can live this out in your world.

TAKE A HIKE

I want to be Your hands
I want to be Your feet
I'll go where You send me
I'll go where You send me

Remember the day you became a Christian? You realized your sin was always going to keep you away from God, and you understood that Jesus was your only hope. So you agreed to turn from sin and believe that Jesus died and rose again for *you*. You decided to put your faith in what Jesus did to get you into heaven with God forever. Then you accepted the fact that you were part of God's family.

That was a huge day. And you didn't need your hands and feet for any of it. It all happened behind your eyeballs and maybe with the words you said in prayer. And then heaven celebrated the fact that another lost one had been found (see Luke 15:7).

That's not the finish line, but way too many Christians stop right there. They're satisfied with the understanding and the believing and the being in God's family. That's enough for them: "Thanks for including me; I've got my ticket. See you in heaven!" Those people don't really want to be Jesus' hands and feet on earth, because it's *hard*. (Check out John 15:18-20 to see what Jesus says about following Him.)

Once you decide to follow Jesus and be His rep on earth, you're going to be busy. Jesus was constantly on the move. Want to know what a day with Jesus would look like? Pray, walk, meet with people, be with people all day, maybe eat, go to sleep, and repeat. Walking and doing. It's exhausting even just *reading* about it. It wasn't only stuff that He talked about and believed in His head; it sank down into His heart and found its way out through His hands and feet. He was about doing what He came to do.

And that's what He wants for His followers. So strap on your hiking boots, grab a pair of work gloves, and let's go. Before we get started, though, let's find out what you know about the places Jesus went and things He did during His time on earth.

SEVEN QUESTIONS

1. **True or False:** Jesus' parents never got frustrated with where Jesus went.

2. **True or False:** Because He was God, Jesus never went to church. Church was anywhere He showed up.

3. **True or False:** Jesus did physical labor with his hands.

4. **True or False:** Because He was holy, Jesus was careful to avoid physically touching people.

5. **True or False:** Jesus never went anywhere He wasn't invited.

6. **True or False:** Jesus never ran away.

7. **True or False:** Jesus only hit people in self-defense.

1. PARENTAL PAIN

Have you ever come home from somewhere to find your parents completely freaked? Maybe you didn't tell them where you were going or they didn't get a message. But they'd been calling your friends and the neighbors. They'd been praying. They were just about to call the police and the hospitals when you came strolling through the door, humming a little tune.

What happened? Did they pounce on you with a combination of anger and relief? Did they hug you and yell at you at the same time? Did they pepper you with questions about what you were up to?

Same thing happened to Jesus. Every year, Jesus' family (and almost everyone else in the country) would take a trip to Jerusalem for the Passover feast. At the time, they lived in Nazareth, where Jesus grew up. Nazareth was about sixty miles from Jerusalem, and there wasn't exactly a tour bus to get down there. So everyone in town would form a big caravan and hike down there over several days, camping each night on the way.

When Passover ended, the caravan started the return trip to Nazareth. Jesus must have been a pretty responsible twelve-year-old, because His folks just assumed He was with the group. At the end of the first day, they started looking for Him. Beginning to panic, they asked all the relatives and friends, "Have you seen Jesus?" Nobody had.

Now in full freak-out mode, they hiked all the way back to Jerusalem, looking high and low for their boy. Finally, they got back in the big city, went to the temple, and found Jesus sitting and talking with the religious teachers.

Mary walked up to Him and said, "Why have You done this to us? Look, Your father and I have sought You anxiously" (Luke 2:48). Jesus basically told her she should have known He would be there. "Did you not know that I must be about My Father's business?" (verse 49). That must have confused everyone, because they thought Jesus' dad was a carpenter. They didn't really understand that He was the Son of God and that hanging out in the temple was a logical thing for Him to do.

Jesus' number-one priority was to do His heavenly Father's business. He wasn't focused on pleasing His earthly parents or His friends or anyone else. Even as a twelve-year-old, He knew He had to obey His heavenly Dad first.

It's easy to build our lives around someone else's plan for us — Mom, Dad, a couple of friends. As Jesus' feet, we can't follow any path that doesn't come from God.

On the other hand, part of following God's plan is obeying and honoring our parents. Jesus did that too. Even though His parents didn't "get" Him (see verse 50), He still honored them by going home with them and being "subject to them" (verse 51). He didn't let His parents define His life purpose, but He obeyed and honored them until He was on His own (and then some).

If we're going to be Jesus' feet, that's got to be our path too.

2. SHOWING UP

Jesus' feet regularly took Him to the synagogue, the church of the Jewish religion. Did He have to go? No — He was God. He didn't need to sacrifice for His sins, and He didn't need to be taught by the religious leaders. But still He participated. Why?

One reason was just to obey His Father. He wanted to honor God's instructions to the Jewish people to follow the Law. Part of that included going to the church. Another reason might be that Jesus went to be involved with His Jewish brothers and sisters. Maybe He built relationships there.

Yet another reason Jesus participated in temple life was to challenge the leaders and the people to honor God. Twice He showed up at the temple in Jerusalem and basically caused a violent scene.

Here's what happened. It's Passover again. About eighteen years have passed since Jesus was twelve and His parents were frantic. This time, Jesus made the trip to Jerusalem with His disciples, His step-brothers, and His mom.

One part of Passover was that people had to bring an animal sacrifice to the temple to cover their sins. Most had to buy one when they got to Jerusalem because they traveled from so far away. And some didn't have local money, so they had to exchange their currency for the right stuff and then buy an animal.

When Jesus showed up and found all of this happening in the outer courts of the temple, He got angry. The temple was meant to be holy, not a marketplace full of animals and "money-changers." So He made a whip and drove all the animals out. He turned over the currency-exchange tables and dumped all the money on the ground. Then He said, "Take these things away! Do not make My Father's house a house of merchandise!" (John 2:16).

God also calls you and me to follow our feet to church and meet regularly together (see Hebrews 10:25). He calls us to be involved in that community by encouraging and serving each other. He wants us to work as well together as the parts of the human body do (see 1 Corinthians 12). And He asks us to follow Jesus' path of challenging each other to live right (see James 5:19-20).

Being Jesus' feet and hands on earth will take us deep into the hearts of our local churches.

HANDS AND FEET IN ACTION

Susan and I had worked together in the same pizza place for nearly six months. I felt as though all I ever heard from her was "Jesus this" and "Jesus that." To be quite honest, it was tiresome. I mean,

I had real problems, and I didn't need to hear the same bit about Jesus every time I wanted to talk about my problems.

Still, Susan insisted Jesus was the answer I needed. She told stories about her life and how Jesus had helped her so many times before. Usually, I would tune somebody out when they started with their "Jesus talk," but Susan started getting through. She was so real about everything. Upon examining her life, I found she and I were really about even as far as life's little problems went.

Susan just had something that I did not have. After a while, I was really able to see how it had affected her life. She never seemed to panic, never seemed to get down about things that would drag most people to the ground, and always wore a smile. I saw that, and I wanted it.

A few months later, I was thinking about all of this on a trip one night. And it just hit me: I needed Jesus. That very night, I got saved. I attribute a lot of that decision to Susan. Every day she would remind me of how wonderful her God is, and every day she would preach to me. Well, she was right. I've never looked back.

Lots of people preach to others with their words. They call it "witnessing." While many people may have witnessed to me and preached to me with words, Susan preached to me with her life. It made a huge impact. I am ever grateful to her for not being ashamed of the gospel.

—JOSH, PLANETWISDOM.COM USER

3.   HARD   WORK

Jesus' earthly dad, Joseph, was a carpenter. Jesus learned the job from Joseph and went to work. Way before Jesus was known in Israel for His miracles and His teaching, He was known in His hometown as a carpenter (see Mark 6:3).

That means Jesus worked at a regular job doing physical labor with His hands. And *that* means He had to show up on time, keep commitments, do the job right, and charge people a fair amount for His time and materials.

Does that seem strange? Is it weird to think of Jesus working long hours measuring, sawing, hammering, and building things? Is it weird to think of Him spending so much time *not* teaching, healing, and traveling?

Sometimes when people set out to follow Jesus and reach out to the world, they get frustrated that they still have to go to work at secular jobs eight hours a day to pay the bills. They wonder why God doesn't just bless them with a bunch of money so they could spend all their time serving Him.

But maybe God *wants* us to work. Maybe hard work is a way for us to imitate God by creating things or serving people or bringing order to our world. Jesus could have just created enough money to pay all the bills so He could start His public ministry before He was thirty. But He didn't. He must have had a reason to work for several years in the family business.

Have you ever thought that being Jesus' hands on earth might mean doing your job really well? It might mean spending hours and years at something that doesn't seem very spiritual just to pay the bills. Being Jesus' hands might mean never going into "full-time Christian work."

Hard work also teaches us discipline, which we need in order to follow Jesus. It teaches us to use our time well and to make the most of our hours, also important parts of following Jesus. And secular jobs often give Christians a chance, in a natural setting, to meet and build relationships with people who don't know Jesus. They get to see our hope in God up close, and we get a chance to point them to Jesus.

Being Jesus' hands on earth means getting to work.

4. HOLY TOUCHING

The culture Jesus grew up in wasn't like ours. We like our "personal space." Most of us get nervous if someone gets within two or three feet of our bodies. We get especially nervous when strangers touch us. And there's nothing wrong with that. Jesus' culture was just different.

Nonsexual touching was a big part of Jesus' relationships with people, especially when He healed people who were sick. Usually, He would touch them or they would touch Him (see Luke 18:15; Matthew 14:36). A lot of the people Jesus came into contact with were considered "unclean" by Jewish Law. That means that Jesus would have to stay away from His friends and family when He touched unclean people. He didn't care. He touched people with horrible skin disease (leprosy), people caught in sexual sin, and some of the worst people around — the tax collectors.

At a meal during yet another Passover in Jerusalem, Jesus washed His disciples' dirty, stinking feet with His own hands (see John 13:5).

And John, probably Jesus' closest friend, leaned up against Jesus' chest as they sat on the floor during the meal. (Chairs weren't popular at the time.)

So what? What difference does it make if Jesus was a "toucher"? The point is that He wasn't afraid to get up close and personal with people. He didn't shy away from human contact. He got dirty.

Some of us would like to be able to reach out to people of the world without getting too close to them. We don't really want to smell them or let them get to know us beyond the surface. We want our faith to stay clean, and by reaching out, we know it's going to get dirty. That's normal, but to be Jesus' touching hands on earth, we're going to have to get past those thoughts.

To really touch the lives of those around us, we've got to let go of the fear of getting too close, of people thinking we're stupid, of feeling other peoples' pain. We've got to be willing to let our lives mix with the lives of others so they can see our hearts and we can see theirs. What do you think we meant when we said this book was about "dirty faith"?

Being Jesus' hands on earth means touching people — it means that our faith gets dirty.

.

5. READY OR NOT

You can divide the world into two kinds of people: initiators and reactors. It feels a lot safer to be a reactor. You wait for others to do something, and then you decide how to respond. And sometimes that makes a lot of sense.

But Jesus was mostly an initiator. He took action even when nobody asked Him to or *wanted* Him to. His feet took Him where He was needed — even if the people there didn't know it.

The religious leaders didn't invite Jesus to come and clean the money-changers out of the temple. He did it because it was the right thing to do. The people of Jesus' hometown who had rejected Him once already didn't invite Him back a second time. But Jesus went back anyway because He knew they needed Him.

Probably the best example of Jesus going where He wasn't invited was the woman at the well in Samaria (see John 4). The Samaritan people were not purely Jewish. Their ancestors had intermarried with non-Jews. Of course, that was against the Jewish Law. The Samaritans also worshiped God differently than the Jews did.

For all of these reasons, the Jews had nothing to do with the Samaritans in order to avoid being thought of as unclean. Some Jews would even walk miles and miles out of their way just to avoid coming across any Samaritan towns. Jesus, on the other hand, walked right into Samaria (see John 4:4).

Besides that, men in Jesus' time didn't start conversations with strange women. It just wasn't thought to be proper, and women were not considered equal to men. So when Jesus walked into a Samaritan town, sat down at a well, and started a conversation with a Samaritan woman, He was breaking all the rules of His society. And He definitely had *not* been invited.

What was the result of this little detour and these conversations? The woman and many people in her town became Jesus-believers (see John 4:41). Jesus took the initiative instead of waiting for the opportunity to come to Him.

It's easier to wait, and sometimes opportunities to be Jesus to people *do* come to us. But being Jesus' feet on earth often means taking action before you're asked. You don't always have to wait for permission.

HANDS AND FEET IN ACTION

THE MISSION YEAR FILES

My roommate Ginny and I were walking home from church, and we decided to stop by Darla's house to invite her to dinner. Instead of finding her at home, we ran into her down the block from where she lived. She was a nervous wreck. The friend she had been staying with had been evicted and didn't tell her.

Darla had to pack her stuff up at the last minute and had nowhere to live. Some friends offered to let her stay one night at their place, and they were in the car waiting for her. Everything she owned was in a shopping cart shoved into a very visible space between two houses.

While she was quickly telling her story, I was praying, God, what do we do for this woman? We aren't allowed to let her stay in our house or even our yard, but there must be something we can do. *Darla's next words were the answer to my prayer.*

"I don't expect you to take me into your house, but will you put my stuff in your yard so no one messes with it?" We agreed. As we gave each other a hug, she began to cry. Then she got into the car and drove off.

Two nights later, Darla came to the door. She wanted to get some of her clothes. I kept her company as she went through her stuff in our backyard. I asked how she was. "Good, considering the circumstances," she said. "It was warm last night when I slept in the park."

My roommates and I called everywhere we could, trying to find a shelter Darla could stay at. I invited her inside and fixed her a plate of food. She complimented my cooking, and we shared some recipes as we waited. When we couldn't find an open shelter, we figured that the least we could do was let Darla use our shower. She was thankful for the opportunity and took quite a long time. When she left, we were worried she'd have to spend another night in the park.

I saw Darla a few days later. She was sitting on someone's porch. She came up to me and hugged me through the black metal bars of the fence. She wasn't quite right. I could tell she'd been involved in something wrong.

Still, when she introduced me to the people around her, she said I was her friend. Maybe I am the closest thing to a friend she's had in a long time. Maybe she doesn't have anyone to share her feelings with. Maybe she has no one to ask how her day's going and to listen to her answer. Maybe she doesn't have someone who remembers her birthday or her favorite kind of ice cream.

Given what she's involved in, maybe I shouldn't associate with her because I'm a Christian and I'm trying to be recognized as such in my neighborhood. Or maybe that's exactly why I should spend time with Darla — because that's exactly what Christians are supposed to do.

—DENISE, MISSION YEAR VOLUNTEER

6.   RETREAT

Toward the end of Jesus' three years of public ministry, He was becoming very unpopular with some people, especially the Jewish religious leaders. They hated that He was claiming to be God's Son and doing miracles they couldn't do and especially that so many people believed Him. Before long, they wanted Jesus dead.

Jesus was forced to use His feet to run for His life several times (e.g., John 10:31-42). He had to slip away before the religious leaders could catch Him and have Him stoned to death.

It looks like that leaves us with two possible interpretations — either Jesus was afraid or He was a quitter. Shouldn't He have stayed in those places in order to keep preaching until they "got" Him? No. Jesus understood it wasn't His time to die yet. It was all about timing.

Being Jesus' feet on earth sometimes means knowing when to leave a situation, not just knowing when to show up. Yes, sometimes it's our job to take a risk by standing for Jesus when we know there will be opposition. And sometimes it's our job to walk away from opposition until the time is right to boldly stand against it. Jesus was never afraid, but He picked His battles.

How do you know when it's time to take a stand and when it's time to move on to a different opportunity? That's where wisdom comes in. To have Jesus' sense of timing, you need God's kind of wisdom. And He offers it freely just for the asking. See James 1:5 for more about finding that kind of wisdom.

7. NOT EVEN IN SELF-DEFENSE

Martial arts are huge right now. And they're a great way to get in shape and learn how to master your body. Some martial arts emphasize that you should never strike another person — except to defend yourself. Makes sense.

Jesus took a much tougher position. While talking to a group of people who had been living under Roman rule and had seen their fellow Jews beaten and killed by their enemy, Jesus said this: "Love your enemies, do good to those who hate you, bless those who curse you, and pray for those who spitefully use you. To him who strikes you on the one cheek, offer the other also" (Luke 6:27-29).

Doesn't sound right, does it? Most of us have been raised in a society that says, "Conquer your enemies. Defeat those who hate you. If someone hits you on the cheek, hit him back hard enough that he can't hit you again." And while it might be the government's job to defend its citizens, how do we respond to Jesus' teaching in our personal life? Does it take more guts to hit someone back, or to let him hit you again? Does it take more strength to love an enemy, or to hate one?

Being Jesus' hands on earth includes what we *don't* do. Jesus' speech about loving and not hitting sounds good, but did He have the guts to put it into action?

If you've read the description of His crucifixion, you know He did. Jesus created the world. He could have eliminated all of His enemies with a thought. He could have called down an army of angel warriors to torch Jerusalem. He could have used His own hands to strike dead everyone who touched Him.

Instead, the Son of God let them beat Him and whip Him and push a crown of thorns down on His head. He let them lead His feet from one place to another. He used His hands to carry His own cross up to the "Place of the Skull" (see John 19:17). And finally, He allowed His enemies to drive spikes into His hands and feet as they nailed Him to the cross.

When you think about it that way, being Jesus' hands and feet on earth is the hardest thing we are ever going to do. It's the hardest thing we're ever going to *think* about doing, because it means being willing to give up our lives for Him as He gave up His for us.

YOUR HANDS, YOUR FEET

Still want to be Jesus' hands and feet in your world? We hope so. We also hope you're beginning to see how hard it will be and how much you're going to have to give up to live a life like His. But how could you pass up the opportunity of seeing God at work in your life and the lives that you come in contact with? You'll begin to see lives changing, and the reward will be huge.

Think about all the places your feet take you: school, the mall, friends' houses, church, new places, familiar places, scary places, and maybe some places you wish now you'd never been. How can you represent Jesus in those places? Now think about all the different things you do with your hands: work, eat, write, wash, touch other people, play instruments, and hold small children. How can you do what Jesus did?

Let's dig a little deeper and find out about some of the people Jesus went to and touched during His time on earth.

CHAPTER THREE

ONE PERSON

And I try, yeah I try
To touch the world like You touched my life
And I find my way
To be Your hands

Human beings like to count and measure stuff. How many people go to your church? How many are in the youth group? How many got saved last year? How many mission trips have you been on? How many homeless people did we feed at the outreach?

Not a thing is wrong with counting or knowing the numbers. The problem comes when we start measuring our success at being Jesus' hands and feet on earth by the numbers of people we reach instead of by the people inside those numbers. Jesus came to reach out to specific individuals who needed Him, not just to save "the masses."

He told a story to make this point (see Matthew 18:12-14). It was about a shepherd who had a hundred sheep. He cared about his sheep so much that if even just one was lost, it was worth leaving all the other sheep to go on a journey into the mountains to save the one that got away.

Why? Were sheep so expensive that it was worth a risky and maybe pointless rescue mission for 1 percent of the flock? Not likely. It's probably because that one sheep had personal value to the shepherd.

He cared about that sheep. That's why he was happier about finding the lost one than he was about the ninety-nine safe back at home.

Jesus felt deep compassion for each individual He touched. He wasn't trying to accumulate followers. He wasn't keeping a tally of the people He had convinced to believe in Him. He was looking for and rescuing one lost person at a time. As His hands and feet on earth, it's our job to do the same thing.

Before we talk about how to do that, let's see how much we know about some of the specific people Jesus went to and touched during His time on earth.

SEVEN QUESTIONS

1. **True or False:** Jesus only healed people to prove who He was.

2. **True or False:** It's easier to heal people than to forgive them of their sins.

3. **True or False:** Jesus condemned all the Pharisees and would have nothing to do with them.

4. **True or False:** Jesus knew things about people that they hadn't told Him.

5. **True or False:** Jesus didn't give people second chances once they had blown it.

6. **True or False:** Jesus especially valued little kids.

7. **True or False:** After Jesus was arrested, His outreach ministry was over.

1. FEELING WITH

Jesus' ability to heal the sick and blind and deformed *did* help prove to the world that He was the Son of God. But sometimes Jesus healed people just because He was overcome with sadness for their pain. He loved them and wanted to make them better.

One example is a man who had leprosy. Leprosy is a contagious disease that, over time, causes a person's skin and extremities to die and fall off. In Jesus' day, there was no cure or effective treatment. (Today there are drug treatments for people, but in some parts of the world, it's still a problem.) People with leprosy had to stay away from healthy people and yell out, "Unclean! Unclean!" anytime someone got close to them.

But this guy walked right up to Jesus, kneeled down in front of Him, and very simply stated his faith in Jesus' power: "If You are willing, You can make me clean" (Mark 1:40).

Mark wrote that Jesus was "moved with compassion." He loved this bold man, and He hurt for him. Then Jesus did something nobody else in His time would ever have done (for fear of catching leprosy): Jesus put His hand on the man and said, "I am willing; be cleansed" (verse 41). And just like that, the man was healed. And just like that, Jesus was made unclean! He allowed His faith to get dirty.

Because Jesus didn't heal the man to prove who He was, He warned the guy not to tell anyone what happened. But the former leper couldn't keep his mouth shut. He had to tell everyone what Jesus did for him.

Being Jesus' hands on earth means we need to learn how to have some of Jesus' heart on earth. Are you moved with compassion for people in pain? Does your heart hurt for the lonely and sick and abused? If nothing ever moves us to feel with the people around us, we're not very likely to get involved in their lives.

But if we can learn to feel the pain of those who don't know Jesus, we're more likely to reach out to them and touch them with God's love. As you come in contact with people who don't know Jesus, ask yourself what you'd be feeling and thinking if you were living their lives. What would it be like to walk a day in their shoes? Allow your heart to fill with compassion. It's at that moment that you'll talk to them about Jesus – He can heal their hurting hearts.

2. FULL FORGIVENESS

Imagine being paralyzed. Maybe you had an accident skiing or riding a bike. You couldn't move anything below your neck. Your friends and family were great about taking care of you, but you longed to be able to walk and run and take care of yourself.

Still, if you were given the choice between being completely healed and going to heaven, which would you pick? The only choice that makes sense is an eternity of freedom. It's by far the greater gift (even if you would really like to walk *right now*).

One man came to Jesus in exactly that condition. The word was out: Jesus was healing people with just a touch. Suddenly, Jesus was swamped with the sick, the hurting, and the dying. Because of the crowds, it got really hard to get to Jesus, especially if you were on a bed carried by four of your friends.

Fortunately, this paralyzed man had some creative (and determined!) companions. They climbed up onto the roof of the building Jesus was in, busted through it, and lowered their immobile friend right in front of Jesus. They must have really believed that Jesus could help the man.

But when Jesus saw the man and realized how much faith the group had, He didn't heal the guy. Instead, He said, "Your sins are forgiven" (Mark 2:5). And if that had been all Jesus had done, it would have been the greatest gift the man could have ever hoped for. Only God can forgive sin, and God had just forgiven his.

But to prove Himself to the religious leaders who were thinking that Jesus shouldn't say He could forgive sins, He also healed the man's body. The once-paralyzed man grabbed his bed and walked out of the building to meet his friends.

What does that mean for us as Jesus' hands and feet on earth? We can offer help—food, medicine, clothing, a listening ear, a shoulder to cry on—to the hurting. But if that's all we do, we're missing the point. We've got to take the next step and let them know they can be forgiven for their sin and can spend forever in heaven with God.

Even if we could meet every physical and emotional need of the lost ones in our lives, we're not imitating Jesus if we don't tell them the good news of salvation. Being Jesus' feet on earth means delivering His message of hope as well as His heart of compassion.

3. PATIENT TEACHING

Do you know of others who are really smart and have a hard time believing in Jesus because none of the other really smart people they know believes? Maybe Jesus intrigues them, but they just can't get past the opinions of their friends and teachers.

Nicodemus was just such a guy (see John 3:1-21). He was a Pharisee and a member of the Sanhedrin, the highest-ruling body of Jewish religious leaders. Most of those men eventually hated Jesus and worked together to get Him crucified. That's why Nicodemus didn't want anyone to know he was visiting Jesus.

Nicodemus believed Jesus was sent from God, but he didn't believe that Jesus was the Messiah. He'd heard Jesus teach and had seen Jesus' miracles. He wanted to know more, but he was afraid of what the other Pharisees would say. So he sneaked to a secret meeting with Jesus behind closed doors.

Did Jesus turn Nicodemus away for being a coward? Did He condemn Nicodemus for not coming to see Him sooner? Did He mock Nicodemus's lifestyle or lack of faith? Nope. He just patiently explained the gospel. In fact, what Jesus told Nicodemus is probably the clearest explanation we have from Him of how to become a Christian.

As "little Christs" on earth, we have to be ready to explain the gospel whenever others are interested — without judging or condemning them. Even if they don't get it at first, even if they mock us or seem afraid to believe, our job is to do just what Jesus did — tell them the truth in love the best we can and leave the decision up to them.

Are you ready to tell the good news about Jesus to others if they ask? What can you do to *get* ready? What if the last person on earth you ever expected to be interested in Christianity came to you and asked about it? Would you be ready to tell the simple truth without judging and leave the response to him or her? As Jesus' hands and feet, that's our calling.

HANDS AND FEET IN ACTION

THE MISSION YEAR FILES

I met Ronald, who's fourteen, about two months ago. He was getting off the bus at a stop near our house. He had a little-boy grin and was kind of shy. I started having more conversations with him on the bus and at the bus stop.

One day, I was supposed to go to an Oakland A's game with the guy down the street. He didn't show up, and nobody I called could go. My last option was Ronald. I didn't really know him or his family, but I decided to give him a try. After I talked to his aunt — she asked me all kinds of questions — Ronald was allowed to go.

That night, Ronald and I had a great time, even though my Yankees lost. We talked and made comments about each other's team (he was rooting for the A's). Ronald even asked the girl sitting next to me — who I didn't know — to give me her phone number. I was so embarrassed, but she did give it to me. I didn't call her. That night at the ballpark started a great relationship between Ronald and me.

Ronald had just finished his first year of high school. He was taking summer classes because he was kicked out of school for the first semester. He had gotten into an argument with a teacher and then started skipping classes. That's also why he lives with his aunt and grandmother. He used to live with his mom, stepdad, brother, and sister. He hates his biological father for leaving, and he's mentioned that his dad tried to kidnap him.

However, Ronald clearly loves his brother and sister. You can tell by the way he interacts with them. Although he has a filthy mouth, Ronald knows when it's appropriate to be polite. He also loves to read. Those last two qualities are hard to find in an inner-city kid.

We've been to the park a few times to play basketball or play catch with the football. We've gone to the library together and to the mall to play video games. We have fun doing those things, but my favorite times with Ronald are when we just sit on his porch and talk. We talk about all kinds of things — the future, family, food, sex, hobbies, school, etc. We just talk about life. Those conversations have allowed me to share my faith in bits and pieces.

One day, Ronald asked me if I was a virgin. I quickly responded with a "heck, yeah." Ronald just started laughing. Then he asked how old I was. I told him I was twenty-two. Then he laughed harder and said, "That has to be some kind of record!"

He said most kids in the city lose their virginity between the ages of eleven and thirteen. I said, "Hey, it's hard work keeping this body from having sex for twenty-two years." Ronald kept laughing, but I was able to tell him a little of why I was still a virgin. God called me to a life of purity, so I committed myself not to have sex until I was married. He took that well and changed the topic.

That's how God guides most of our conversations, giving opportunities for me to listen and then to share. Ronald's a very special kid to me. He's the reason I'm here.

—MARK, MISSION YEAR VOLUNTEER

4. GETTING TO KNOW YOU

In the last chapter, we mentioned the Samaritan woman Jesus met at the well, but we didn't really discuss what she and Jesus talked about. If you remember, Jesus was breaking most of the rules of society just by being in her town and talking to her. But what was His approach to offering her eternal life (see John 4:1-42)?

This woman was automatically suspicious of Jesus. From her side of the conversation, it's clear she knew what she believed and what the Jews believed. She tried to start up the ancient argument with Jesus, but He wouldn't bite. Instead, Jesus kept bringing the conversation back to what she needed.

He offered her a water that would keep her from ever thirsting again (see verse 14). He showed that He knew her by describing all her husbands and boyfriends (see verses 17-18). Then He revealed that He was the Messiah that she'd been waiting for (see verse 26).

When she went to tell her friends about Him, she wasn't convinced yet, but she was curious: "Come, see a man who told me all the things that I ever did. Could this be the Christ?" (verse 29). Eventually, she and many others in her town believed in Jesus.

Jesus obviously cared about and understood this woman. He wanted to save her and her friends. He knew her well enough to hook her curiosity and avoid arguing with her. He revealed the sin in her life without condemning her. Then He told her the simple truth.

Unlike Jesus, we don't have the ability to know everything about someone the first time we meet him or her. So as Jesus' feet, it's going to take us a little longer to get to know people enough to approach them in the way that works for them. But because everyone is valuable, it's worth our time to build those relationships.

Then we can appeal to their curiosity. We can tell them about God's answers to their pain. And we can offer them the hope of salvation through Jesus.

5. GO AND STOP

The Jewish religious leaders who didn't like Jesus were getting desperate. They wanted to be able to point to something He had said or done that went against the Law. Then they could justify killing Him.

This time they thought they had Him (see John 8:3-11). They brought a woman caught in the act of having sex with a man she wasn't married to. Some Bible teachers speculate that it might have been a sting operation. The Pharisees might have set a trap for her to catch her and bring her to Jesus.

Because Jewish Law said a woman caught in adultery should be stoned to death, they were using the woman as bait. If Jesus said she should be stoned, the people would see Him as harsh and condemning. If He said to let her go, they would see Him as too soft on sin and disobeying the Law.

So what did Jesus do with His hands? He wrote in the dirt and ignored the Pharisees. Then He said the one thing they didn't have a comeback for: "He who is without sin among you, let him throw a stone at her first" (verse 7).

Even in their enthusiasm to get Jesus, the Pharisees knew they couldn't condemn the woman. They realized they had their own secret sins. As one writer said, you could almost hear those stones hitting the ground, one by one, as the group walked away. Then Jesus forgave the woman and told her to "go and sin no more" (verse 11).

We're also guilty of sin. We've been forgiven through Christ's death for us, but we still struggle with our desire to do wrong. As deliverers of the gospel, we have a choice: We can be like the Pharisees, constantly catching people in their sinfulness and conveniently forgetting about our own while we warn them they're going to hell, or we can be Jesus' hands and feet, telling sinners about the mercy God gave to us in spite of our own sin. We can offer hope and freedom from hell through God's grace because we've been given the same thing ourselves. We can spread the word of God's forgiveness. That's what Jesus did.

6 . LET THEM COME

Being Jesus' hands and feet can take you to vacation Bible school, an Awana Club, or the nursery at your church. You might have thought those jobs were only for people who can't do "real ministry." Think again.

One day, lots of people wanted to bring their kids to Jesus so He could touch them and bless them. The disciples, maybe thinking Jesus' time could be better spent teaching or healing sick people, put a stop to that. "Jesus can't see you now. Maybe if you come back in a few years . . ."

When Jesus heard what the disciples had done, He wasn't happy. He said, "Let the little children come to Me. . . . Whoever does not receive the kingdom of God as a little child will by no means enter it" (Mark 10:14-15).

Some studies show that as many as 80 percent of Christians got saved when they were eighteen or younger, most when they were twelve or younger. Jesus welcomed the children and held them and blessed them. He knew that it takes childlike faith to believe in Him. People do get saved as adults, but they still have to believe like children.

So don't let anyone say that telling your friends about Jesus is somehow less important than being a missionary to Africa. This is one way to catch people at the best possible time of their lives—when they're still young enough to believe easily.

7. SUFFERING EVANGELISM

You wouldn't think Jesus would have had any time to reach out to an individual after He was arrested. All of the beating and whipping and getting grilled by the Jewish leaders and Pilate would have made it difficult. On top of that, He was about to die in terrible pain.

Still, there it is in Luke 23:39-43. Crucifixion was a regular thing in Roman society. It happened all the time. On the day Jesus was killed, two other men were being executed on the same hill. One mocked Jesus, which you might expect from a criminal. He said, "If You are the Christ, save yourself and us" (verse 39).

But the other criminal saw a different picture as they hung there. Even though it was Jesus' worst day ever and He had been beaten beyond recognition, this criminal believed Jesus was the Son of God. So he asked to be saved—not from being killed, but from eternal death (see verse 42).

Jesus promised: "Today you will be with Me in Paradise" (verse 43). Jesus met the spiritual need of one last person before He died to meet the greatest need of all people.

The Bible doesn't promise that Christians won't suffer. In fact, suffering is one of the ways we follow Jesus as we live out our lives here. He suffered, and we may suffer for Him. But sometimes, as with Jesus and the criminal, it's our suffering that lets lost ones see our hope for life in heaven with God. That's why Jesus' disciple Peter wrote, "Always be ready to give a defense to everyone who asks you a reason for the hope that is in you" (1 Peter 3:15).

When someone you love dies, when your parents decide to get a divorce, when your family runs into financial troubles, when you're persecuted for what you believe — those are the times the world around you gets to see what you're really trusting to give meaning to your life. When they see you still have hope even though your world is crashing down around you, they'll want to know why.

Will you be ready to share the reason for your hope?

YOUR MISSION: PEOPLE

Still want to be Jesus' hands and feet? We hope so. We also hope you've seen that it's not about all the people you reach out to over the course of your whole life. It's not about saving crowds of people by pointing them to the Savior. It's about the one person in your life right now who needs to see Jesus. It's about the friend who just can't get over that bad breakup. It's about the little kid next door whose parents are splitting up. Maybe it's about someone in your very own family. Can you be Jesus' hands and feet in that one person's life today? That's all God's asking for.

HANDS AND FEET IN ACTION

THE MISSION YEAR FILES

Trish lives upstairs from me. I know her from hearing her yell "Shut up!" at her kids as they wake up crying in the morning. She's seen me out on my roller blades and mentioned the two of us going roller-blading sometime. So for a couple of weeks, I stopped by her door to see if she had time to get away. Finally, a few Saturdays ago, she did. She then invited me to her apartment to hang out while she got ready.

Though as many as five adults and six children live there at any given time, they don't have much. I noticed a couple of dressers and bunk beds in the two bedrooms. But where I sat out in the living room on the crumb-infested carpet, there was only an ironing board, a TV stand, a TV, and a VCR. Two of the kids were sleeping on big throw pillows. At first, I figured this was where they napped. I later discovered this was where they slept at night too.

Trish and I chatted while she fixed her hair. When Trish got her roller blades out, I offered to spray them with some lubricant while she finished getting ready. Then we slapped on our wheels, and off we went!

We rolled toward the park, talking about the neighborhood and our memories of roller-skating as teens. At the park, we went to the tennis court area. Then we really started to talk. Trish told me she's thirty-one and the mother of two boys. Her youngest son is named after his dad, who died last year. Trish is living with her sister because she doesn't have a job or place to stay. She used to sleep with a guy just to have a place to stay. Trish also told me her sister's boyfriend was a drug dealer and that she had once been addicted to heroin.

I was amazed by how much personal information she told me about herself so soon. I didn't know whether to believe it all, but it gave me a chance to tell Trish about some things in my past that aren't so pretty. I also told her how God has so faithfully and graciously brought me through those things.

Since that first visit, I've dropped by and hung out with Trish and her children quite a bit. She's amazed every time I offer to help her clean the apartment or watch the kids. I'm amazed how God has given me not only a way to connect with Trish but also the energy to really get to know her and care for her.

This woman I used to resent for the way she treats her children is now someone whose life I've had a chance to impact with the love of Christ. It might not look as though much has changed. Trish still yells and swears at the kids. She still comes and goes with a variety of men. She still abuses alcohol and marijuana. But one thing has definitely changed: Trish now has a neighbor who's determined to be a conduit for God's transforming love into the lives of her and her children.

I don't think she knows how much I pray for her. I don't think she's aware yet that when she leaves me with her baby and the other kids, I go into hyper-affection mode and sing to them about how much Jesus loves them. I don't think she knows quite yet that I believe God's got an entirely different way of life waiting for her —if she wants it.

But what Trish does or doesn't do isn't in my hands. What is in my hands is the challenge to be obedient to His call to be the most loving neighbor to Trish that I know how to be. It's been a challenge that I've delighted to see God backing up with faithfulness along the way.

—JILL, MISSION YEAR VOLUNTEER

CHAPTER FOUR

AT YOUR SERVICE

I've abandoned every selfish thought
I've surrendered everything I've got
You can have everything I am
And perfect everything I'm not
I'm willing, I'm not afraid
You give me strength

In a scene of a movie about life in England a hundred or so years ago, one woman was asking another about her role as a servant to the rich people of a large household. Didn't she ever get tired of them bossing her around? Didn't she ever resent having to clean up after them and fetch things for them?

The servant said no, that being a servant was her calling and she was good at it. She knew the people she was serving. She knew when they would be hungry, and she had the food ready. She knew when they would be tired, and she had the beds turned down. She knew when they would want something, and she would have it for them before they asked. As a servant, her joy was to meet the needs of the family.

That attitude doesn't hit home with us these days, does it? We usually do work for one of three reasons: we have no choice, we really like the job, or we need the money. The whole idea of working just to meet another person's needs sounds crazy.

Surprise! Jesus said His main mission on earth was to serve other people. And (ouch!) He called us to do the same thing (see Matthew 20:28). For us, at least, that means changing everything about how we look at the world.

Instead of making it your goal to be in charge, serve the person in charge. Instead of making it your goal to take care of yourself and leave everyone else alone, help take care of others, even if they don't help you in return.

A big part of us says, "Ick." How about you? You might be saying, "I need some help figuring out what being a servant means and how to jump in and do it. I need some help even *wanting* to be a servant." Before we dig in, though, let's see how much you know about what Jesus said and did to serve others.

SEVEN QUESTIONS

1. What is the best way for Christians to treat others?

   a. As equals

   b. As followers

   c. As more important than ourselves

   d. All of the above

2. When it came to thinking like servants, Jesus' disciples . . .

   a. Were naturally good at putting each other first.

   b. Always focused on meeting Jesus' needs.

   c. Sometimes looked for their own glory first.

   d. Wore little tuxedos with white gloves.

3. To be great in God's kingdom, what do you have to do?

   a. Lead at least a dozen people to Christ.

   b. Preach fabulous sermons.

   c. Feed the hungry and visit people in prison.

   d. Become a great servant.

4. Why did God make you talented in certain areas of your life?

   a. So you could get rich and famous

   b. So you could really enjoy your time on earth

   c. So you could be better than someone at *something*

   d. So you could invest your talents in serving Him

5. Who was Jesus serving when He performed miracles?

   a. His Father

   b. The people He was helping

   c. The whole world

   d. All of the above

6. Is sharing our money and stuff with other people a way of serving them and God?

   a. Yes, of course.

   b. No, giving is a completely different thing.

   c. I sure hope not.

   d. What money? What stuff?

7. What's the best way to serve Jesus?

   a. Obey the Father.

   b. Follow Jesus' path on earth.

   c. Love each other.

   d. This is too easy — all of the above.

1. AFTER YOU

"Honor one another above yourselves" (Romans 12:10, NIV). It's easy to skim right over that, but let's think about what it means: "Treat other people as though they're more important than you are." That's like wearing your shoes on the wrong feet. It just feels wrong. In our current society, we're taught to think of everyone as equals. Nobody's better, nobody's worse — we're all the same.

But part of Jesus' upside-down plan for people who want to be His hands and feet is that we treat people like He did — like they matter more than we do. That goes not just for your parents and your friends, but also for your little brothers and sisters, the gang at work, your teachers.

Does that mean that all those people are better than you? Nope. It's not about actual importance; it's about how we treat each other. It's like the army. If you're a private in the army, you treat everyone above your rank with respect (whether you like them or not). You do what they ask, and you salute when they walk by.

Paul was saying we should treat everyone like they have a higher rank than we do. We should acknowledge their significance as people. We should listen respectfully. We should do whatever we can to meet their needs. In short, we should be each other's servants. It's what Jesus did: "Being in the form of God, [Jesus] . . . made Himself of no reputation, taking the form of a bondservant" (Philippians 2:6-7).

Check out this passage from John 13:3-17 (MSG):

> Jesus knew that the Father had put him in complete charge of everything, that he came from God and was on his way back to God. So he got up from the supper table, set aside his robe, and put on an apron. Then he poured water into a basin and began to wash the feet of the disciples, drying them with his apron. When he got to Simon Peter, Peter said, "Master, you wash my feet?" Jesus answered, "You don't understand now what I'm doing, but it will be clear enough to you later."
>
> Peter persisted, "You're not going to wash my feet—ever!"
>
> Jesus said, "If I don't wash you, you can't be part of what I'm doing."
>
> "Master!" said Peter. "Not only my feet, then. Wash my hands! Wash my head!"
>
> Jesus said, "If you've had a bath in the morning, you only need your feet washed now and you're clean from head to toe. My concern, you understand,

is holiness, not hygiene. So now you're clean. But not every one of you." (He knew who was betraying him. That's why he said, "Not every one of you.") After he had finished washing their feet, he took his robe, put it back on, and went back to his place at the table.

Then he said, "Do you understand what I have done to you? You address me as 'Teacher' and 'Master,' and rightly so. That is what I am. So if I, the Master and Teacher, washed your feet, you must now wash each other's feet. I've laid down a pattern for you. What I've done, you do. I'm only pointing out the obvious. A servant is not ranked above his master; an employee doesn't give orders to the employer. If you understand what I'm telling you, act like it—and live a blessed life."

If we were to let ourselves serve only our interests (be our own hands and feet on earth), our desire would be to gain a big reputation and become important and respected. As Jesus' hands and feet, we've got to turn that attitude off and think like a servant. Easier said than done, as we're about to see.

HANDS AND FEET IN ACTION

THE MISSION YEAR FILES

She lives across the street from us. She often wears sunglasses, even if it's not sunny. And many times, she's loudly angry about something. We never really know what kind of mood she'll be in. To be honest, I'm a little intimidated by her. Her name is Bonnie, and I'm excited about my relationship with her. Let me tell you why.

We live in a neighborhood that is half African-American and half Hispanic. We're the only white people, and we don't fit in. In fact, white people in this neighborhood are usually associated with the police. Until recently, Bonnie was convinced that's who we were. That made it tough to get to know her.

I play with Bonnie's eleven-year-old daughter almost every day, and I talk to her niece. But I couldn't break through to have any kind of a conversation with Bonnie herself. Until a couple of weeks ago, I would have been happy just with not getting any more angry glares from her. My attempts to say hi on the street and stop by her apartment didn't seem to help at all. Then one evening, Bonnie voluntarily said hello to me.

I couldn't believe it! I excitedly told the rest of my teammates that they would never guess who had just said hello to me (and I was right). Then last week, Bonnie asked me if I knew how to cook gumbo. This woman who used to think I was a cop was practically asking for my help with something! Her question led to an actual conversation. I don't remember what we talked about, but I was so excited. Since then, she seems to feel really comfortable around us.

It gets better. The doorbell rang this morning, and there was Bonnie, offering us some of her leftover gumbo. I was so stunned I could hardly speak at first. After my initial surprised reaction, Bonnie came in and left us with a kind, neighborly gesture.

I'm realizing a few important things lately. First, God is the one doing all the things that matter, not me. When I simply stand back *and let Him take control . . . wow! Second, even when I don't see results right away, that's okay. If I'm being faithful to what God wants me to do, that's all that matters. And if what God wants me to do is keep saying hello and keep being loving to a neighbor who doesn't seem to like me, that's what I need to do. Third, I feel like I'm being given so much more than I give others.*

—*MARGIE, MISSION YEAR VOLUNTEER*

2. DISCIPLES, NOT EXAMPLES

The twelve disciples had been following Jesus for three years, but they still didn't quite understand what He was up to. They knew He was the Son of God. They believed in Him and wanted to follow Him. But they had a hard time understanding that He wasn't going to set up His kingdom on earth right away. The idea that He would die soon hadn't clicked with them.

They didn't get it right even after Jesus said out loud, "When we get to Jerusalem, I'm going to be killed and rise again three days later" (see Mark 10:33-34). You can tell they didn't get it by what James and John said to Jesus one verse later: "Teacher, we want You to do for us whatever we ask" (verse 35).

Huh? Jesus says, "I'm about to die," and they say, "We want a big favor!" Obviously, they weren't tracking. But Jesus was patient: "What do you want?"

Then James and John laid on Him the biggest favor ever requested in the history of the universe. They asked to sit on either side of Him when He became king. In the culture of Jesus' time, sitting right next to the most important person made you the next most important person. James and John were asking to be number two and three in Jesus' kingdom.

It gets worse. We know from the same story in Matthew 20 that James and John's *mom* came with them to ask Jesus this favor. You can almost hear her at dinner the night before: "What are you two doing with your lives? What—besides worn-out sandals—do you have to show for three years of walking around with Jesus? When Jesus finally becomes king, I hope you at least get good positions in His government. In fact, you should go ask Him right away before He gives the good spots away to someone else."

Even after three long years with Jesus, James and John didn't have a clue what it meant to be a servant. They were looking out for their own statuses. Jesus told them that not only could He *not* give them what they asked for, but also that they were going to go through the same suffering He was about to go through. Eventually, they would learn through hard times that following Jesus didn't mean gaining power. In fact, it meant the opposite.

So, what *does* it take to get a high-status position in God's kingdom? Funny you should ask.

3. THE GREATEST

In His response to James and John's request to be great in God's kingdom, Jesus gave all of the disciples some mind-bending advice: "Whoever desires to become great among you shall be your servant. And whoever of you desires to be first shall be slave of all" (Mark 10:43-44). Under that arrangement, the assistant janitor at your school would be telling the principal what to do, the high-school intern at Microsoft would be signing Bill Gates' checks, and army generals would be saluting eighteen-year-old privates. Jesus' kingdom sounds like an interesting place.

So who's going to be the greatest in Jesus' kingdom? Well, Jesus. Why? Because Jesus is the greatest servant who ever lived: "The Son of Man did not come to be served, but to serve, and to give His life as a ransom for many" (verse 45). Jesus came to earth as a slave to us all and then, in His most humble act, died on the cross for us.

If we're going to be Jesus' hands and feet on earth, we're going to have to humble ourselves too. We're going to have to lower our heads and start serving each other the way He served us. We'll need to get our hands dirty, just like Jesus did, and "wash each other's feet." That kind of service to God and others really does pay off in the end.

Like Jesus said, great servants become great in God's kingdom. Look what happened to Jesus after He humbled Himself: "Therefore God also has highly exalted Him and given Him the name which is above every name" (Philippians 2:9).

When we humble ourselves and trust God to do what's best with our status, He'll do the same for us: "Humble yourselves under the mighty hand of God, that He may exalt you in due time" (1 Peter 5:6).

Want to be great in God's kingdom? Want to be Jesus' hands and feet on earth? Look around and find someone for you to serve. Let's talk about how to do that.

4.   TALENT   SHOW

So once we're ready to serve God and each other, what exactly do we do? Once we've agreed that we need to have an attitude of "After you," what do we actually spend our time doing? Do we all sign up for the nursery or become missionaries or start washing each other's cars?

Jesus taught that it depends on what God has given you. He told a story about a master with three servants (see Matthew 25:14-30). He gave one servant five "talents" of silver to manage for him. (A talent was a weight used to measure valuable metals or money.) He gave the second servant two talents. And He gave the last servant one lonely talent.

Then the master left, and servants one and two became businessmen. They invested the money and were soon able to double it to ten talents and four talents, respectively. But servant number three was so afraid he'd use the money in the wrong way that he just buried it in his backyard.

Of course, the master was thrilled with the first two guys. But the last servant got into serious trouble for not even trying to make a little profit off of the money he'd been given.

Sounds more like a business class than a story on being a servant, doesn't it? And in a way it is. Jesus' point was that God has given each of us a package of skills, abilities, finances, and other resources. He wants us to use what we've got and what we're good at to serve Him and others. When we use it, our talents grow as they get transferred into the lives of other people.

What are you good at? Basketball, writing, listening, building things, washing cars, babysitting? How can you use your talents to serve God and other people? You don't have to serve others with something you don't have. Serve them with what you do have. Get creative like the servants with the talents. Find new ways and places to invest your life that will have benefits in the lives of your friends, church members, and neighbors.

Being Jesus' hands and feet on earth means serving others by giving yourself — including your talents and abilities—away.

HANDS AND FEET IN ACTION

THE MISSION YEAR FILES

Gina, a middle-aged woman, came into the emergency shelter. I was working as an advocate, and she poured out before me on the dirty dining room table the paperwork destruction of her life. It was a ten-page lawsuit for the custody of her only son and her single treasure on this earth.

Gina had no way of finding a lawyer to defend her from the father of her eight-year-old boy, and only two weeks remained until the hearing. She swept her tangled red hair back and wept while telling the story. She said that she tried not to think about the desperate measures she would have to take while going on the run with her son if things didn't work out.

I led her back to the office and started calling legal assistance agencies. She said this was more care than anyone had shown to her in this nightmare of hers. She beamed with gratitude through newly dry eyes. She caught me off guard with a hug and a comment about my being an angel.

—CAL, MISSION YEAR VOLUNTEER

5. IT'S A MIRACLE

One way that Jesus served the people around Him was by performing miracles. He turned water into wine to serve the host of a wedding. He healed the sick and raised the dead to serve their obvious need. He made a few fish and some bread stretch to satisfy the hunger of thousands of people.

"That's great," someone might say, "but I can't exactly do miracles to serve others. I'm not as powerful as Jesus." That's not totally true. Jesus says, "The person who trusts me will not only do what I'm doing but even greater things, because I, on my way to the Father, am giving you the same work to do that I've been doing. You can count on it" (John 14:12, MSG). If you're a Christian, you do have supernatural power. As we mentioned in an earlier chapter, the Bible tells us that every person who trusts in Jesus for salvation receives one or more of these spiritual gifts (see 1 Corinthians 12).

What's the point of those gifts? "Each one should use whatever gift he has received to serve others" (1 Peter 4:10, NIV). God feels so passionately about our serving each other that He even gives us the supernatural power to do it.

If you have the gift of teaching, you have the supernatural ability to explain the truth of God's Word in a way a nongifted person can't. If you have the gift of helping, you can supernaturally help others do what needs doing in a way a nongifted person couldn't even if they wanted to. If you have the gift of encouragement, you can supernaturally lift a person's spirits better than people without that gift can. (You can find lists of the spiritual gifts in 1 Corinthians 12; Romans 12; Ephesians 4; and 1 Peter 4.)

Our job in the church is to be Jesus' hands and feet to each other by using our gifts. In a way, we're using God's power to do little miracles in each other's lives. And when we do *that*, together we become Jesus' whole *body* here on earth.

5.   FINANCIAL   SERVICE

Money is a powerful force in the world. Governments are built around the way they create and distribute money. Status in our society is often determined by how much money a person has. Many marriages crumble because of disagreements over money. How we look at money says a lot about who we are as people.

It's not surprising, then, that Jesus talked about money all the time. He wanted to make sure that people who were going to be His hands and feet understood two things about money: how to think about it and what to do with it. It's also not surprising that both of those things have to do with being a servant.

First, Jesus said not to live for money. How many people do you know who have organized their whole lives around making money? They sacrifice everything in order to get enough money to get what they want. Then they have to make more money to keep what they've got. Jesus called these people servants—servants of money. The problem with that is you can only serve one thing at a time: "No one can serve two masters; for either he will hate the one and love the other, or else he will be loyal to the one and despise the other. You cannot serve God and [money]" (Matthew 6:24).

Servants of God—those who want to be Jesus' hands and feet on earth—will have to give up serving money. It could mean that you'll be willing to live with less money if serving God keeps you from making more. Didn't see that one coming, did you?

So, all servants of God and other people are poor, then, right? Nope. Many God-servants have *lots* of money. In fact, most of the God-servants in America are rich by worldwide standards. And some of them are really, really rich by *anybody's* standards. That's not wrong as long as the money isn't controlling them. In fact, that brings us to the other thing Jesus taught about money (and stuff we own).

We can use our money and our stuff as a way to serve God and others. Jesus praised a poor widow who gave away all she had left in the world to serve the church (see Luke 21:3-4). And when one boy was willing to share his lunch to serve hungry people, Jesus took it and miraculously used it to feed thousands (see John 6:1-14).

You have money and belongings. Even if you don't have much, sharing what you do have is another way you can be Jesus' hands and feet on earth.

7. I WILL FOLLOW

We've talked about how to be servants of God and servants of the people in our lives. But is there a way we can serve Jesus Himself? Yup. In fact, it's what we've been talking about in this whole book. Jesus asked those who wanted to serve Him, the Master Servant, to *follow* Him (see John 12:26).

In other words, we serve Jesus by being like Him — by being His hands and feet on earth. Do you get why that matters? Jesus was so focused on serving people and serving His Father that the only way to serve Jesus is by serving people and serving His Father. You can't separate serving Jesus from serving everyone else—it's the same thing.

SERVICE PLAN

So what's your service plan? Do you have one? Do you have ideas for using your talents, spiritual gifts, and money to serve God and others? Or are you still struggling with the idea that being a servant means treating everyone else like they're above you? Do you catch yourself thinking like James and John about how to become a VIP in your world?

Becoming a servant might be the hardest part of being Jesus' hands and feet on earth, especially when you realize that His greatest act of servanthood was allowing Himself to be killed on that cross for us. Following in His steps can only lead to dying ourselves. Like everything else about being a Christ-follower, it's *hard*.

Still want to be Jesus' hands and feet on earth? We hope so. Fortunately, this hard path isn't one we walk alone. God gives us the power to do it through His Holy Spirit. We just have to say "yes" and keep walking.

CHAPTER FIVE

FATHER FOCUS

> *This is the last time*
> *I turned my back on You*
> *From now on, I'll go so*
> *Send me where You want me to*

When you talk to counselors, it's amazing how many issues they deal with that come down to people's fathers. It's hard to imagine a more important relationship in our early lives than the one we have with our dads.

Having a gentle and strong father who is a man of integrity and character (and who loves Mom) makes it much easier for us to become healthy, well-balanced people. And we all know what having missing or neglectful or angry dads can do to kids. Even years later when a person is on his own, he can struggle with the aftermath of having a hurtful papa. Most dads fall somewhere in the middle. And most of us have strengths and weaknesses in our lives because of the man our daddy was at the time he was (or wasn't) raising us.

Jesus also has a Father. You *cannot* understand who Jesus is and was on earth if you don't know about His most important relationship—the one He had with God the Father. And you can't be Jesus' hands and feet on earth unless you also have a relationship with His Father.

We've noticed that some Christians don't really like to talk about the Father. Maybe because they didn't have healthy relationships with their own dads, they prefer to focus on Jesus and pray to Jesus and worship Jesus. But that's not the example Jesus set for us. He came to provide a way for us to have a relationship with the Father.

In this chapter, you'll see how you can copy Jesus by relating to the Father like He did when He was on the earth. First, let's test what you know about Jesus' most important relationship.

SEVEN QUESTIONS

1. True or False: Jesus needed the Father.

2. True or False: Because Jesus and the Father are one, Jesus never needed to pray to the Father in public or in private.

3. True or False: The Father cares whether or not we worship Him.

4. True or False: Jesus relied on His own power while He was on earth.

5. True or False: Jesus made His own decisions while on earth.

6. True or False: Jesus talks to the Father about you.

7. True or False: Jesus' Father is also your Father.

1. THE SOURCE

All little kids eventually go through a stage in which they start saying to Mommy and Daddy, "I can do it by myself. Don't help. I can do it." They want to put on their own shirts. They want to brush their own teeth. They want to ride their bikes by themselves. It's an important part of growing up.

Jesus never said anything like that about His Father because Jesus knew He was never going to "grow up" and move away from Him. In fact, Jesus said exactly the opposite of "I can do it myself." Check out John 5:19-20:

> *The Son can do nothing of Himself, but what He sees the Father do; for whatever He does, the Son also*

does in like manner. For the Father loves the Son,
and shows Him all things that He Himself does.

Jesus understood that all His knowledge, all His supernatural power, and all His authority to be God on earth came from His Father in heaven. Without the Father, there would be no Son.

Jesus didn't show up on earth on a rogue mission from heaven. He came only because the Father sent Him (see John 3:16). Jesus knew the Father loved Him, and He came to point everyone who would listen back to the Father.

As Jesus' hands and feet on earth, our job is to be like Him by growing *dependent* on the Father. It never makes sense for us to say to God, "I've been serving You for a while. I think I can handle this one on my own." It's only logical to copy Jesus and say to God, "I won't say any words or take any actions or walk any steps that don't come straight from You, Father."

Becoming more like Jesus is opposite of growing up and away from our parents. It's like saying, "Please hold the bike and run alongside me. Please help me brush my teeth. Please tie my shoe for me." Like Jesus, we can't do anything that really matters without the Father.

2. COMMUNICATION

Jesus and God are one, but that didn't stop Jesus from praying to the Father all the time. We know that He would go off by Himself and talk to His Father, sometimes late into the night (see Matthew 14:23-25). He had an especially long conversation with God the night before He was crucified (see John 17).

You get the sense from Jesus' priority on prayer that it was a huge part of His life, especially when He was overly busy or facing a hard situation. Take a look at the following examples:

> *Very early in the morning, while it was still dark, Jesus got up, left the house and went off to a solitary place, where he prayed. (Mark 1:35, NIV)*

> *But Jesus often withdrew to lonely places and prayed. (Luke 5:16, NIV)*

> *One of those days Jesus went out to a mountainside to pray, and spent the night praying to God. (Luke 6:12, NIV)*

It also seems from reading Jesus' prayers that talking to the Father wasn't a ritual or a religious exercise for Him. Jesus talked to the Father from His heart about what was on His mind. He talked to the Father as though they had a relationship and an ongoing conversation that never really stopped.

What does that mean for us? A major part of following Jesus is spending time talking to the Father, just like Jesus did. He got comfort and direction by talking with God. So can we. Does that mean it's wrong to pray to Jesus too? Not at all. But Jesus told us to pray to the Father.

Remember Jesus' "model prayer" when the disciples asked Him how to pray? Look at how He told them to pray: He told them to start out by saying, "Our Father in heaven" (Luke 11:2). He wanted the disciples (and us) to have a relationship with the Father like He did.

Being Jesus' hands and feet on earth means talking to the Father.

HANDS AND FEET IN ACTION

Through the Internet, I've seen God's power reach across time zones, countries, and cultures to touch lives. I consider the Internet my mission field, and I try to be an encouragement to friends. Like people seen in "real life," sometimes the encouragers need encouragement.

Sometimes when I'm almost falling apart, someone will say something that seems to come straight from God. He uses others to help my spirit even when they don't realize it.

After a rough day, I got online. A friend was also online, and he complimented me.

"You're too kind," I responded.

"You can't be too kind," he said. For a glistening moment, I understood the love of Jesus. He wants me to show His kindness to people. That's what I needed to hear, and I thanked God for my friend.

Once, I was preaching to someone far away who wanted to become a Christian. He commented on my enthusiasm: "You're not like the others. They are like lazy guild members who do nothing. But you're not like them."

I beamed and continued leading him to Christ. (He eventually became a Christian.)

I was talking to a friend and she said, "You're the only one who cared enough to make sure I was walking the road God wanted for me. I am forever grateful."

Aren't friends great? They're God's way of encouraging the encouragers. What a great way to be Jesus' hands and feet in someone's life.

— KAITLYN, PLANETWISDOM.COM USER

3. WORTHSHIP

No, we didn't write that word above this line with a lisp. Our English word "worship" was originally (a long time ago) spelled "worthship." It means to acknowledge what something is worth.

Over the last few years, worship has become hugely popular. Lots of Christian artists have recorded and sold whole albums of worship songs. The sales tell us that Christians are hungry to worship God through music.

Some of our worship songs are directed at Jesus, which is great. Jesus obviously deserves our worship. In heaven, one of the songs we'll sing talks about how worthy the Lamb is to be praised (see Revelation 5:12). The Lamb is Jesus. We'll spend eternity worshiping Him.

But Jesus also said we should specifically worship the Father. Remember that story about Jesus' conversation with the woman at the well? The Jews and the Samaritans disagreed about the right place to worship God. One thing Jesus said to the woman is that from that point on, it wouldn't matter *where* you worshiped the Father. What mattered is that you *did* worship the Father: "The true worshipers will worship the Father in spirit and truth; for the Father is seeking such to worship Him" (John 4:23).

Jesus said the Father wants us to worship Him in spirit (meaning from the deepest parts of ourselves, not just with money or things) and in truth (meaning to be authentic and not fake our worship).

Music is just one way to worship the Father. Paul wrote that giving our whole lives to God is an act of worship (see Romans 12:1-2). Worship is anything we say, write, sing, do, or don't do that points to how worthy our Father truly is.

Everything about Jesus' life was worship of the Father. And it's a big part of being Jesus' hands and feet ourselves.

4.   TRUSTWORTHY

When you fly in an airplane, you don't think about making the plane take off or land or go in the right direction. Sometimes a flash of "What if . . . ?" might cross your mind when you remember images on the news of planes going down. But because you can't do even one little thing about it, what do you do? You let it go. You completely trust the pilot and air traffic control to safely get the plane where it's going. Sometimes you may even sleep.

That's how Jesus trusted the Father. Remember all that stuff from the last chapter about being a servant? When Jesus humbled Himself and became a servant to every person who ever lived by dying on the cross like a common criminal, He was trusting that the Father would lift Him up. And the Father did (see Philippians 2:5-11).

We're putting a lot of trust in the Father, too. If we're going to serve those around us, we trust Him to make sure we get taken care of. If we're going to give up living for money, we trust Him to make sure we have enough to eat and somewhere to live. If we're going to walk the hard road of being Jesus' hands and feet on earth, we trust the Father to give us the power to do that (and He promises that He will).

Jesus said that when it comes to the Father, we don't have to worry: "Look at the birds of the air, for they neither sow nor reap nor gather into barns; yet your heavenly Father feeds them. Are you not of more value than they?" (Matthew 6:26).

Being Jesus' hands and feet on earth means trusting the Father to meet our needs so we can focus on meeting the needs of others.

5. NOT MY WILL

Have you ever played that game where you get blindfolded and then someone leads you through a maze or a building by shouting instructions to you? "Turn right!" "Keep walking!" "Stop! Stop!" It can be really scary, especially if your "leader" isn't good at giving instructions.

When you're blindfolded, your only choice is to listen to the instructions and do what you're told. If you can't see, it doesn't make sense to say, "I don't like that instruction; I think I'll go this way instead."

Jesus' relationship with the Father was just like that, except Jesus wasn't blindfolded. He just trusted the Father and did nothing except what the Father told Him to do. In fact, Jesus said that doing the Father's will was His food (see John 4:34). Fulfilling God's will was His mission. It satisfied Jesus and kept Him going.

In our relationship with God, we're more like the blindfolded person in that game, except that we usually don't realize how blind we are. Even when we have no idea what's coming next, we think we're in control of our lives. Of course, we're not. All we can be sure of is what God has told us in His Word, which is huge because we see how He's worked in the lives of other people. That allows our trust in Him to grow.

Even then, figuring out the Father's will for our specific lives can be hard. Paul gave a three-step plan (see Romans 12:1-2): First, give up your own will and turn your life over to God as a living sacrifice; second, don't follow the path of the fallen-down world around you; and third, be changed from the inside out by renewing your mind with God's Word, and then you'll be able to figure out what God's will is.

Most of us get stuck on that first one – giving up our own wills. It's hard and it hurts, especially when God's will clearly goes in the opposite direction. But that's what Jesus did, isn't it? When He was about to die, He prayed in the garden: "Abba, Father, all things are possible for You. Take this cup away from Me; nevertheless, not what I will, but what You will" (Mark 14:36). Jesus was a living sacrifice.

Being Jesus' hands and feet on earth means doing the Father's will, even to the point of death.

6. PRAY FOR ME

Did you know that Jesus talked to the Father about us when He was here and He still talks about us now that they're in heaven together?

On the night before He died, Jesus prayed a long prayer asking the Father take care of His disciples (see John 17). It's really touching because you can tell Jesus knew He was going to die. He knew He wouldn't be around much longer to take care of those men He loved.

But He didn't just pray for the *disciples*; Jesus also mentioned *us*: "I do not pray for these alone, but also for those who will believe in Me through their word [That's us!]; that they all may be one, as You, Father, are in Me, and I in You; that they also may be one in Us, that the world may believe that You sent Me" (verses 20-21).

How comforting to know that Jesus was thinking of us and asking the Father to help us even on one of the worst nights of His life. And it gets better. Right now, Jesus sits on the right hand of God praying for us (see Romans 8:34). Jesus still loves us. He's still working for us.

As Jesus' hands and feet on earth, we can continue His work by praying for one another. How often do we pray for our friends and family? How often do we pray for our leaders and church members? How often do we pray for strangers? It's hard to keep it up, isn't it?

But prayer for your brothers and sisters—and for nonChristians— is something you can do to be like Jesus anyplace and at anytime.

7. OUR FATHER

Whether you have a lousy dad or the best dad on earth, he's not your *only* dad. When you trusted in Christ as your Savior, you were adopted into God's family (see John 1:12). You have a right to be called a child of God now. That's huge.

After Jesus rose from the dead, one of the first people He showed Himself to—even before the disciples—was Mary Magdalene. Mary had been a faithful follower of Jesus ever since He cast seven demons out of her (see Luke 8:2).

I don't know what kind of relationship Mary had with her dad. Maybe it wasn't very good, because she ended up so open to demonic influence. But it's clear she loved Jesus deeply. She'd been devastated by His death and just couldn't stop crying when she found His empty tomb. She thought His body had been stolen.

When He spoke her name outside of the tomb, she recognized Him and called out, "Teacher!" We assume she must have moved to hug Him, because Jesus said this to her: "Do not cling to Me, for I have not yet ascended to My Father; but . . . I am ascending to My Father and your Father, and to My God and your God" (John 20:17).

Did you see what Jesus did there? He started by saying, "My Father," and then He included "your Father." He wanted Mary to know that His Father was now hers as well. His God was now hers too. She couldn't hug Jesus anymore, but she now had a perfect Father to serve and talk to and love and live for. She had an "abba" (the Greek word for "daddy") who would always love and care for her.

How's your relationship with your Abba? Do you talk to Him? Do you worship Him? Do you work to do His will? That's what Jesus' mission to earth was all about. He wanted you to get to know His Father.

FAMILY MISSION

We can't be Jesus' feet on earth unless we walk with the Father. We can't be Jesus' hands on earth unless we let the Father direct everything we do.

Still want to be Jesus' hands and feet? We hope so. Yes, it's hard. But knowing that our Father provides for us and directs us and gives us the power to keep going makes it easier. And knowing that we're just one of millions of people in His family makes it less lonely.

The Father loved Jesus and He loves us too. He won't ask us to do anything too hard for us. And He won't lead us to anyplace where He can't meet our needs. We can be Jesus' hands and feet the same way Jesus was — by relying on the Father.

HANDS AND FEET IN ACTION

THE MISSION YEAR FILES

As soon as I walked into Mama Jean's house, she opened up her arms for a hug. She told me how worried she was for me. She didn't remember my name, but that's normal. She remembers my face and refers to me as her baby. She told me she would adopt me if she could.

My team was going to give her our Christmas tree the next day, and she was talking about that. She even got up and did a short dance and sang a song about how God is good. We talked about many things, as always. She told me a funny story about her sister.

I think Mama Jean and I brighten each other's day every Saturday. She tells me how she used to just sit on the couch all alone and cry, and now I come to keep her company and she looks forward to my visits.

Mama Jean inspires me with her hospitality. Today, a homeless lady who Mama Jean had obviously helped before came over to use her phone. Mama Jean gladly let her use her phone. I see her helping her family and others in need every week. She says, "Well, you never know when I might need a piece of bread or somewhere to stay, so I help them when they need it."

Mama Jean is really the one who needs looking after. She drinks all the time, she has already survived a stroke, and she's recovering from cataract surgery. But she keeps giving of herself. My team is giving her a special birthday dinner. She's already looking forward to that.

—JOAN, MISSION YEAR VOLUNTEER

CHAPTER SIX

HANDS AND FEET YOU'VE NEVER HEARD OF

I finally have a mission
I promise I'll complete
I don't need excuses
When I am Your hands and feet

Some people have funny ideas about being Jesus' hands and feet on earth. They think you've got to be a preacher or a recording artist or a youth speaker or a songwriter to really touch people's lives. You've got to be famous and cool.

We've found almost the opposite in our lives. Often, the best ministry comes through one-on-one conversations and relationships with people—just as it did for Jesus. In fact, sometimes being famous gets in the way of those "small" conversations. Sometimes being a "big star" makes it harder to be Jesus' hands and feet with just one person.

The point is that you don't have to wait for a career in order to be Jesus' hands and feet. Every Christian can be Jesus' hands and feet in the lives of family, friends, and neighbors.

Right now, ordinary people have the power to do incredible things when they just offer themselves to God to be used as Jesus in the life of the person standing right next to them. No microphones, no three-point outline, no sixty-city tour, maybe not even words—just you and another person and the love of Jesus. That's huge.

The Bible describes lots of ordinary people—not apostles, not prophets, not even teachers—who were used by God to do powerful things for Him in the lives of those around them. Before we meet a few of them, answer these questions to find out what you know about what it takes to be extraordinary for God.

SEVEN QUESTIONS

1. True or False: Praying for people isn't ministry.

2. True or False: Taking care of people isn't ministry.

3. True or False: Helping someone else do ministry isn't ministry.

4. True or False: Visiting people in prison isn't ministry.

5. True or False: Just doing the right thing when you have the chance to isn't ministry.

6. True or False: Sharing your house and stuff isn't ministry.

7. True or False: Encouraging people isn't ministry.

1. PRAYER WRESTLER

Of course, praying for others is a way to be Jesus' hands and feet on earth. As we read earlier in this book, prayer is one way Jesus ministered when He was here, and He still prays for us in heaven.

Have you ever heard of a guy named Epaphras? It's okay if you haven't. His name pops up only a few times in the Bible. Although Epaphras was involved in being like Jesus in other ways too, prayer is the thing he's most famous for. Check out what Paul wrote about him to the Christians in a town called Colosse:

> *Epaphras, who is one of you, a bondservant of Christ, greets you, always laboring fervently for you in prayers, that you may stand perfect and complete in all the will of God. (Colossians 4:12)*

Prayer is a ministry anybody can do for someone else at any time. It doesn't take a special gift or the right connections or a sound system. It just takes talking to our Father like Jesus did. But that doesn't mean it's easy.

Did you catch how Epaphras prayed for the people in his church? *Laboring fervently* means Epaphras was "working hard" at praying for others. Another Bible version says that he was "wrestling" in prayer. The Greek word is the same one from which we get "agonizing." For Epaphras, prayer was a workout.

Is prayer ever hard work for you? It can be. Sometimes you don't see any fruit for years! Asking God to help your brothers and sisters in Christ stay strong in their faith and keep becoming more and more like Jesus takes time and focus and energy. It's work, but it's work that pays off in the long run.

James wrote that effective praying gets things done (see James 5:16). God listens to us and responds. Too many people get hung up on the idea that because God is working out His own plan, it doesn't matter if we pray. That's a lie. If it were true, God wouldn't tell us to pray in the first place. His Word wouldn't say that our prayers matter. He wants us to pray, and He responds to our prayers. He doesn't always say "yes," but He always hears and He enjoys giving good gifts to us and to those we pray for (see Luke 11:13; James 1:17).

You don't have to be talented or educated or on a church staff to be a prayer wrestler. All you have to do is start talking to God.

Looking to be Jesus' hands and feet? Try prayer. It's the hardest job you'll have that others will ever know you're doing unless you tell them.

2. THERE FOR YOU

You probably *have* heard the name "Phoebe" even if you've never heard of the one from Romans. The Bible version of Phoebe was more than just a good "Friend." She lived as Jesus' hands and feet just by helping people in really practical ways.

Apparently, she was on her way to help people in Rome when Paul was writing his letter to the Christians in that city. Paul obviously respected this sister a lot. He wrote this:

> *I commend to you Phoebe our sister, who is a servant of the church in Cenchrea, that you may receive her in the Lord in a manner worthy of the saints, and assist her in whatever business she has need of you; for indeed she has been a helper of many and of myself also. (Romans 16:1-2)*

Wow! Nothing like a personal recommendation from the guy God used to write half the New Testament. Phoebe took all those ideas about being a servant that we talked about a few chapters back and she actually *lived* them. She was such a good helper that Paul told the believers in Rome to do whatever she said in order to help her help them.

Do you know anyone with a ministry of helping? When there's work to do, these are the people who show up and get it done. They don't necessarily teach or preach or sing or go to committee meetings. They get the work done. They live as Jesus' hands and feet by being there for others in concrete ways.

By just agreeing to be a helper, you can build a lifelong, practical ministry to the people in your life.

HANDS AND FEET IN ACTION

THE MISSION YEAR FILES

It's been very interesting working at Legal Aid over the past few weeks. Today I worked with an elderly gentleman named Homer. He needed some assistance finding senior citizen assisted-living housing.

Homer was being evicted from his home of twenty years. The new owner "wanted to do some renovation" to the property. Translation: The landlord wanted more money in rent than the old man was able to pay. Because the eviction is taking longer than originally planned, the landlord has cut off the water to Homer's apartment in hopes that it will speed Homer's exit from the premises.

Homer is extremely soft-spoken. The people who run the assisted-living program have informed us that the waiting list for all the available options means it will be six months to a year before Homer can find a home. Homer doesn't have that kind of time. His landlord wants him out now.

Sometimes a negotiation can be reached in which a tenant can stay in his or her current housing until their new unit becomes available. That's what we were trying to arrange for Homer so that he wouldn't end up homeless.

As we were filling out the paperwork, Homer started telling me about his wife and son. He hadn't talked to either for several years.

Now he's ready to make amends with them. Hearing that small piece of his story broke my heart.

I hope that we can help Homer keep his home or find a new one soon.

— JOHN, MISSION YEAR VOLUNTEER

3. BROTHER'S KEEPER

Are there one or two people in your life, maybe not even a lot older than you, who spent time with you one-on-one to help you understand the truth of God better? If so, you're probably really thankful for those people. It's hard to think of a more powerful ministry than mentoring.

It seems like Apollos was an amazing teacher (see Acts 18:24-28; 1 Corinthians 3:4-6). He was great at teaching the truth about Jesus accurately and in a way that people could really get. This guy was definitely going to have an "up-front" ministry.

Aquila and Priscilla were a well-known Christian couple. Aquila was a tent maker and did a little bit of teaching. They both spent time with Paul and became good friends with him. When Apollos came to their town, Aquila and Priscilla were very impressed with his ability. But they saw a hole in his knowledge about Jesus.

So what did they do? Scold him? Turn him in to the apostles? Nope. Instead: "When Aquila and Priscilla heard him, they took him aside and explained to him the way of God more accurately" (Acts 18:26). The original language makes it clear that they invited Apollos to their home. They spent time with him, and they carefully explained the whole truth to him.

This Christian couple saw that Apollos just needed a little direction to make his teaching gift even more powerful. If someone has done that for you, you know what a difference it can make. How can you help a younger brother or sister in Christ get a better understanding of the truth? Is that a ministry God is calling you to do?

4. BEHIND BARS

If you've never spent any time in jail, it's hard to understand how lonely and depressing it can be as the months and years slide by. Showing up to talk to and listen to people in prison is an incredible ministry. Thousands have come to know Christ while behind bars just because believers chose to be Jesus' hands and feet by showing up faithfully to be with them.

Prison worked a little differently back when the New Testament was written. In some cases, prisoners were allowed to have guests come and stay with them to provide meals, service, and emotional support.

Paul wrote his letter to the believers in Philippi from a Roman prison. He might have been locked up in a house at the time. In Philippians 2, he mentioned that Timothy and a man named Epaphroditus were staying with him.

Epaphroditus was a leader in the church in Philippi, but his ministry to Paul was about "just being there." He sacrificed time with his family and friends to meet Paul's needs in prison. He was Jesus' hands and feet to Paul, doing so much for Paul that he got sick and almost died. Paul wrote this about Epaphroditus:

For indeed he was sick almost to death; but God had
mercy on him, and not only on him but on me also,
lest I should have sorrow upon sorrow. . . . because
for the work of Christ he came close to death, not
regarding his life, to supply what was lacking.
(Philippians 2:27,30)

Anyone can do prison ministry. It's all about showing up and providing for people who can't go anywhere. You can do the same for
people in hospitals, in nursing homes, or stuck in their houses. God
calls us to be Jesus' hands and feet to those people by taking His
friendship and love to them.

HANDS AND FEET IN ACTION

THE MISSION YEAR FILES

I've been working as a legal aid. Harold's a fifty-seven-year-old res-
ident at the shelter. He's become a dear friend to me over months of
working with him on voucher extensions and advocating a welfare
entanglement hearing.

A few weeks ago, he was taken to the hospital for pneumonia
and a punctured intestine. One afternoon, I called the hospital just
to talk to him and see how he was doing. The staff told me he was
back in the dorms on bed rest. They suggested I go and check on
him, so I did.

Venturing down the dark and musty hallways to a makeshift
room in the back of the ancient building, I opened the door to see
Harold's familiar eyes peek out from under a grave of shameful

blankets. As I stepped over the debris of this dark lodging to sit down by his feet, he said he had just been thinking about me.

I was able to sit there and listen to him talk about the last week of his life. This time, it was about the hospital and the annoying side effects on his bowel movements. Before I left, I decided to ask if I could pray with him. So I took the hand that I had shaken a hundred times before and held it while I prayed over Harold, his body, and his heart.

—CARL, MISSION YEAR VOLUNTEER

5. DO THE RIGHT THING

Being Jesus' hands and feet isn't always about some specific ministry—sometimes it's about just doing the right thing when the opportunity comes along. The apostle John had a friend like that. His name was Gaius.

John wrote the shortest book in the New Testament as a letter to Gaius. According to John, Gaius spoke the truth about God, he lived the truth he talked about, and he did what was right for both strangers and people he knew (see 3 John 3-6).

In short, Gaius lived like Jesus. His life was his ministry. He didn't need a stage or demo tape—he was the gospel walking around on a couple of legs. People knew Jesus better through Gaius doing the right thing whenever he had the chance.

You've got to know a few people like that—not stars of the Christian world, but men and women who are kind and helpful and live what they believe. Everybody can have that ministry, but not everybody does.

Sometimes being Jesus' hands and feet on earth just means doing the right thing.

6. HOUSE PARTY

A long time ago, Kool-Aid ran a bunch of commercials about that house in the neighborhood where all the kids hang out. They called the mom of that house the "Kool-Aid mom" because she was always happy to have people in her house and she was always ready to share food and, well, Kool-Aid with them.

Do you remember a "Kool-Aid mom" from when you were a kid? Maybe it was your mom or your friend's mom. She always had snacks and didn't mind if you and your friends crashed on her couch. That's called hospitality.

Being a "Kool-Aid mom" (or friend or neighbor or family member) is another way to be Jesus' hands and feet on earth. Hospitality is a great way to be used of God. In fact, the church has always depended on people to do that.

John Mark's mom was a "Kool-Aid mom." She let the church meet in her house. And when Peter was thrown in jail for preaching about Jesus, she let the Christians come to her house to pray for him. God used her house and listened to those prayers—and busted Peter out of prison (see Acts 12:11-17).

Lydia was a businesswoman who also followed Jesus by letting people stay at her house. In fact, right after she got saved, she pretty much demanded that Paul come and stay at her house. She wouldn't take no for an answer (see Acts 16:13-15).

You might not have a house to share, but hospitality is as much about attitude as it is about having a place. You can have a ministry of hospitality just by being willing to share whatever you do have (food, clothes, your car) with others, especially for the purpose of serving Jesus.

Hospitality is a great ministry—and it doesn't require any public speaking whatsoever.

7. GIVING COURAGE

You've probably never heard of Joses, but you might know him by his other name: Barnabas. This guy was so good at encouraging people that the apostles changed his name to one that meant "Son of Encouragement" (see Acts 4:36).

Barnabas isn't famous today for being a great speaker, but God used him in powerful ways because Barnabas was willing to be Jesus' hands and feet to people by encouraging them.

Encourage literally means "to give someone courage." How did Barnabas do that? He believed in people. He stood up for people. He partnered with people to support them and make them look better. You totally can do this at school. You know the people at your school who are constantly picked on? Why not stand up for them? Why not introduce yourself to new kids at school or in your youth ministry?

When Paul had just become a Christian after a career of hunting and killing Christians, Barnabas was the guy who stood beside him and introduced him to the apostles (see Acts 9:27). Barnabas traveled far to encourage new Christians to stand strong for Jesus (see Acts 11:22-24). He and Paul traveled together telling people how to believe in Jesus (see Acts 13-14). And when Paul had a good reason not to trust a guy named John Mark, Barnabas stood up and said, "I believe in this man, and I'm going to help him" (see Acts 15:36-40).

Do you know someone who you would call a "Child of Encouragement"? How real is his or her ministry in your life? How can you be Jesus' hands and feet today by giving courage to the people around you?

ORDINARY HANDS, EVERYDAY FEET

Maybe you've got the gifts and desire to be a powerful Bible teacher or great evangelist or to sing songs of worship to lead people to focus on Christ. If so, great! Go for it!

But if you're pretty sure that's not how God is going to use you, it doesn't mean you can relax and leave "ministry" to others. In fact, living as Jesus' hands and feet in the lives of your family and neighbors can be a big deal. Why? Because that's where people find out if Jesus is for real or not.

Preachers and singers can say the most powerful and beautiful words in the world, but that's all they are — words. Music has a way of getting us excited and energized and helping us to feel close to God. But those are just emotions.

What the world needs to see is Jesus in action in real life. They need to see Jesus under the stress of finals week. They need to see Jesus in the locker room. They need to see Jesus on the job. They need to see Jesus facing disappointment. In other words, they need to see Jesus in you even if you never preach a sermon on just how cool Jesus is.

This chapter has mentioned a few ways to be like Jesus that don't require speaking or singing or anything public. Can you pray? Can you help get the work done? Can you teach truth to a younger Christian? Can you make a right choice about how to live? Can you share your house and stuff? Can you give away a little courage by standing next to a friend?

Then you can be Jesus' hands and feet right now. The world is waiting.

HANDS AND FEET IN ACTION

I was in a terrible accident in a van while traveling from Myrtle Beach, North Carolina, to my home in Roanoke, Virginia. I know Christ's hands were on and with me during my long recovery in the hospital after the accident. One pair of these kind, giving, and loving hands belonged to Chuck Blinkhorn. He read about the accident in a local newspaper. While visiting someone else in the hospital, Chuck decided to stop by my room.

After that first visit, Chuck visited me as often as he could — sometimes weekly, sometimes more. He helped bolster my confidence for regaining myself. He was there, beside God and my family, giving support and encouragement and helping me understand what had happened.

Even more important, Chuck helped me accept the accident and what had happened to me. He helped me understand that, while the accident wasn't a part of God's perfect plan, it had happened because of the sin in the world. But God could still use the accident to further what He planned.

Another life God used as Jesus' hands and feet for me is that of John Purdy. John is the chaplain for the rehabilitation floor at my hospital and one of the most remarkable men I've ever met.

Meeting John is one of my first memories of rehab. It was almost dinnertime, and a loud knock came at my door. I wondered who it could be. Mom wasn't due back till the next day, Dad wouldn't get there until the weekend, and my brothers were at school. In walked the most alive person I've ever seen in a hospital. An aging but still lively man with a glad face and a cheerful smile, John introduced himself and asked if I would be willing to talk about God.

John helped me keep my faith in God strong and growing through some hard trials. He was definitely used by God in my life.

—HELEN, PLANETWISDOM.COM USER

CHAPTER SEVEN

"YOU RUINED MY LIFE"

I want to be Your hands
I want to be Your feet
I'll go where You send me
I'll go where You send me

If you haven't heard it, the strange title of this chapter is the name of a song on our new album, *WorldWide*. It's all about how following Jesus changes everything in our lives. All our hopes, all our dreams, all our plans go out the window. Suddenly, our whole world turns upside down.

Sound harsh? Maybe. But by the time you get to the end of this chapter, it just might sound logical.

There's an old story about the monkey with a jar of grapes. The mouth of the jar was just big enough for him to get his paw through, but when he grabbed a handful of grapes, his fist was too big to get back out through the jar's opening. The monkey had to choose to either have the grapes in his hand but never eat them, or have his paw out and free. He couldn't have both.

We're going to see that following Jesus — really living as His hands and feet on earth — is kind of like that. We can spend our lives grabbing all the good things we can get our hands on, even though in the end none of those things will really satisfy us, or we can let all those things go and use our hands to do His will.

Fortunately, we're not monkeys. That means we have the ability to understand the difference between the two paths in front of us. The question is: Do we have the courage to choose the only path that's worth following?

Before we look at what that means, spend a few minutes on this test to see how much you know about following Jesus.

SEVEN QUESTIONS

1. What does it cost us to follow Jesus?

    a. Cost? We're doing Him a favor. Why should we pay?

    b. He'll take whatever we can give for now.

    c. We should be ready to give up a majority of our lives.

    d. Jesus wants all of us — or nothing.

2. In comparison to our commitment to Him, how did Jesus say His followers should feel about their families?

    a. We should love them a little less than Jesus.

    b. We should pretend they don't exist.

    c. We should hate them.

    d. We should treat them like dirt.

3. Why did Jesus tell us to carry our crosses?

    a. To show that we're dead

    b. To build our arms, backs, and abs

    c. To show that we belong to Him

    d. All of the above

4. How did Jesus predict the world would feel about His followers?

    a. Warm and fuzzy.

    b. He said we'd become celebrities.

    c. He said people will respect us because everybody loves Him.

    d. He said the world will hate us just as it hated Him.

5. After Jesus died, He . . .

    a. Was remembered fondly by His friends and family.

    b. Came back to life and finally started living for Himself.

c. Came back to life with a new purpose.

d. Got out of here as quickly as possible.

6. **What's worship?**

a. Mumbling through halfhearted praise songs from the back of the church

b. Praising God as sincerely as possible with music

c. Willingly giving my whole life to God

d. Both "b" and "c," but a lot more "c"

7. **What's the best thing about this life?**

a. Enjoying the beauty of creation

b. Finding success in work and relationships

c. Becoming more like Jesus

d. That it's over quick and we get to go to heaven

1. LETTING GO

Have you ever done something your mom thought was stupid? Come on, now. Every hand should be up. There you go.

When your mom asked why you did it, did you ever answer, "Well, Johnny did it"? Maybe your friend wasn't named Johnny, but you remember the conversation, don't you? And then your mom would say something like, "Well, if Johnny jumped off a cliff, would you do that too?"

In case you're wondering, the right answer was "no." But Jesus asked His disciples a very similar question (with a much tougher answer). He looked at the men who had followed Him for three hard years and asked, "If I jumped off a cliff, would you?"

Okay, that's not exactly what He said to them, but it's the same idea. He knew He was going to die. So people who wanted to follow Him had to be willing to die too — and not just physically. Here's what He really said:

> *If anyone desires to come after Me, let him deny himself, and take up his cross daily, and follow Me. For whoever desires to save his life will lose it, but whoever loses his life for My sake will save it.* *(Luke 9:23-24)*

So the first question we've got to ask ourselves before signing up to follow Jesus is: Am I willing to lose my life? And we're not just talking about taking a bullet. That would be easier. Jesus was asking us to give up our "living" lives.

What plans do you have for next week? Next month? Ten years from now? Trash 'em. What are your dreams for the future? For your career? For your perfect spouse? Throw 'em out. How about your goals for a comfortable living and a solid education? Forget the whole thing.

Following Jesus means letting Him rewrite your whole agenda for your life. He said, "Deny yourself." That means giving up everything you might have coming to you, everything all the nonfollowers of Jesus will spend their time chasing and enjoying. By your own choice, you're going to say, "I'm releasing my rights to any of it. I'll take what You give, Jesus, and I'll live by Your plan."

Jesus gave up everything. He asks us to do the same. Still want to follow Him? Don't answer yet. It gets harder.

HANDS AND FEET IN ACTION

Mark Stuart's dad, Drex, describes how God has used his life and family as the hands and feet of Jesus on earth.

In November of '89, after being in Port-Au-Prince, Haiti, for about three months, we noticed our daughter was getting very weak and often short of breath. We thought she might have malaria or some other tropical disease. I was on the local Haitian Amateur Radio net one morning and met an American doctor who was help-ing a medical mission in the city. He heard me describe Kelly's symptoms and asked me to bring her to him immediately. Two days later, we were on our way back to the States.

At a hospital in Evansville, Indiana, Kelly, then fifteen, was diagnosed with acute lymphocytic leukemia! What a shock! I was so hurt and angry with God. I said something like, "God, I'm a mis-sionary. I don't have much except for my kids. Now you're going to take one of them from me?"

Jo, my wife, was hurting also, but she looked at me and said, "Drex, for thirty years you've preached that we need to trust God in all situations, good or bad. Now when it's your turn to trust, you're wanting to turn away from Him." She was right. I needed to trust. After praying together, we went into Kelly's room to tell her the diagnosis. The next day, we flew to Memphis, Tennessee, so she could be admitted to St. Jude's Children's Research Hospital.

St. Jude's Hospital was a haven for us. God always knows exactly where we should be. We immediately felt a great sense of relief from our fears when we first entered the building and met

Kelly's outstanding doctors. All we could do was put our trust in them and place them all in God's hands.

The protocol at St. Jude's was to get the patients into remission quickly. They gave Kelly very strong chemo treatments every day for the first six weeks. It took eight weeks, but she finally went into remission. She underwent treatment for the next two years. Kelly became a fighter; she had a battle to win. She entered the challenge headfirst with Christ as her shield. She never lost faith. She seemed to have a constant peace, which made a great impression on many people. She was a walking witness.

A motel room in Memphis was now our home. Family and friends rallied around us. Our network of Christian friends in the States and Haiti covered us in prayer daily. People sent cards, food, and even money. One dear friend, who owned a car dealership in Indiana, sent us a car to use. People from the church we had left, Southern Heights Christian Church in Somerset, Kentucky, came to visit and asked me to return as their minister. They were a concerned and caring group of people. God was taking care of us. It's great to be a Christian in troubled times.

After remaining in remission for ten years, the doctors considered Kelly cured of her leukemia. Kelly is now a registered nurse and assistant director of nursing at a long-term care facility. She has been a tremendous witness to those around her, both young and old. We have seen many lives changed because of her love of the Lord.

We have been willing workers. Jesus has always been there leading and guiding us along the way. When we do question, we just fall back on our much-cherished Proverb: "Trust in the Lord with all your *heart, and lean not on your own understanding. In all your ways acknowledge Him, and He shall direct your paths" (Proverbs 3:5-6).*

My wife and I continue to allow God to use our hands and feet.

—DREX STUART

2 .   FAMILY   PLOT

You might think that following Jesus would mean getting really close to your family, working through all your issues with them, and learning to get along together. Makes sense, but it's wrong.

Jesus said this: "If anyone comes to Me and does not hate his father and mother, wife and children, brothers and sisters, yes, and his own life also, he cannot be My disciple" (Luke 14:26).

Wait a minute, now. Doesn't the Bible tell us to honor and obey our parents? Aren't husbands supposed to love their wives and kids? Didn't Jesus Himself even say that the second greatest command was to love our neighbors as ourselves (which seems like it would include our families)?

"Yes" to all questions. Jesus wasn't talking about the kind of hate that involves treating people badly. Far from it. He was talking about motivation. Why be kind and loving to your family? Why honor and obey your parents? One reason only: Because God said so. Not because they've earned your love. Not because they're good people. Only because you've committed yourself to God.

Sounds cold, doesn't it? Don't ever give yourself away to your family because of *them*— only do it for *Him*.

Sounds like you'd be more committed to Him than to anyone else in the world.

Exactly.

And when following Jesus leads you away from your family, especially your parents, letting them go to follow Him might feel harsh. But He's your only priority now. When He came to earth, He left behind His Father and His home. He asks you to be willing to do the same, even if it hurts your loved ones. Now, you have to be careful here and get counsel from people you trust and who have walked with Jesus for a long time. Check what you're thinking against God's Word and God's people—if they don't line up, ask God to show you clearly what He wants you to do.

This is sounding harder and harder. And we're still not through.

3. CROSS TRAINING

A prisoner who has been sentenced to execution and is living out his last days on death row is sometimes called a "dead man walking."

Jesus knew that He too was a dead man walking. He knew that before long, He'd be carrying His own huge, heavy, wooden cross up Skull Hill to the place of His execution. That's why He said to His disciples, "And whoever does not bear his cross and come after Me cannot be My disciple" (Luke 14:27).

Why would Jesus ask His followers to take up their own crosses every day? Remember all that stuff about giving up our lives? Taking up our crosses is how we make it permanent. Dead men don't go back to their old ways of living. They stay dead. Jesus wants us to be so much His that we never forget we're dead to our own ways of doing things.

Someone dragging around his own execution device has trouble forgetting that he is a "dead man walking." When we remember to pick it up every day, we don't forget that we're as good as dead to ourselves.

There's a second cool idea here. Roman prisoners were forced to carry their crosses through the streets as a public admission that they were guilty of their crimes. The Romans wanted everyone to see that these people had broken the law and were being punished for it. Carrying the cross was like a confession.

So when we "take up our crosses," it's like we're saying, "Yes, I was wrong. God was right. I needed Jesus. I belong to Him now." We're not going to die for our sins, of course. Instead, carrying our crosses is a way of saying that we died with Jesus (see Romans 6). Our sinful selves are dead.

So, what does that look like for you? Maybe you need to stop going to certain websites or downloading all that "free" music. Think about the areas in your life that grieve Jesus, and ask Him to help you put all those old things away.

4. UNPOPULAR

One last hard truth here. Maybe you've noticed this one. The world *hates* Jesus. You might have missed it because so many claim to respect Him and like His teaching. They even make movies about Him.

But the world is not much different than it was when He was here on earth. Okay, the technology and politics have changed, but human beings haven't. And how did the world treat Jesus back then? They killed Him. (Remember, this is the guy you're following.)

Why does the world hate Jesus? For one thing, He's totally inflexible on that whole salvation thing. Many of the rest of the world religions play nice and say you can get to heaven and be with God in lots of different ways. They say, "Our religion is just one great option to salvation."

Jesus said, "No one comes to the Father except through Me" (John 14:6). Not a lot of wiggle room there. And the world hates that Jesus would be so arrogant to say that you can't go to heaven without Him. Of course, it's not arrogant if it's true. In fact, if it's true, it would be really mean not to tell.

But if you tell the world that truth, it's going to hate you just like it hated Jesus. Here's what He said: "If the world hates you, you know that it hated Me before it hated you. If you were of the world, the world would love its own. Yet because you are not of the world, but I chose you out of the world, therefore the world hates you" (John 15:18-19).

The world system hates Jesus so much that you could someday be physically harmed or killed for following Jesus. It's happened over and over again throughout history. It's happening right this minute all over the globe. Following Jesus is risky.

5. ALIVE AGAIN

Okay, so let's review. In order to follow Jesus, you're going to have to lose your life, hate your family, die to your own way of living, and plan on being hated by the world system. Not exactly what you'd expect to see on a recruitment poster, is it?

Obviously, following Jesus is hard. So why do it?

Well, what are your options? How else could you live if you were running your own show? You could spend your life following pleasure, money, fame, power, success, and fun. You might even catch most of them. Then what? Seventy years—eighty if you're lucky—and the show's over.

Maybe you'll do well enough and be remembered fondly by a few people. Maybe you'll get your name in the encyclopedia. But what will you really have lived for? Does following any path but the one Jesus laid down make sense when you realize you can spend your life participating in God's great big plan?

It's true that you're following someone who got killed, and He has asked you to follow Him right over the cliff. But you're also following someone who walked out of His own tomb three days later. Jesus doesn't just ask you to die with Him—He asks you to live in Him (see Romans 6:11).

Once you've died to yourself, Jesus offers you the most amazing, adventure-filled life you could ever imagine. Yup, it's hard—but nothing is more exciting. Remember, Jesus also said this: "I have come that they might have life, and that they may have it more abundantly" (John 10:10).

Christians don't just die—we're born again; we're made new! Paul wrote: "If anyone is in Christ, he is a new creation; old things have passed away; behold, all things have become new" (2 Corinthians 5:17).

When Jesus died, He came back to life with a new mission—to be with His Father and prepare a place for us. When we "lose our lives," Jesus gives us a new mission: "Be My hands and feet here on earth." You'll never find a more exciting purpose.

6. REAL WORSHIP

So what's this alive-again life all about? What are we actually supposed to do with ourselves between here and the exit to heaven? One word: Worship.

Now, wait a minute. We're not talking about breathing your way through praise songs and hymns in church. I'm not even talking about the most amazing, most sincere worship concert you've ever been to. I'm talking about real, 24/7 worship.

What's *that* mean? It means giving God everything you've got, every minute of every day, for the rest of your life. It means letting Him change you from the inside out until your friends who "knew you when" don't even recognize you anymore. It means, in short, becoming that new person He's making you into.

The following will help: "So here's what I want you to do, God helping you: Take your everyday, ordinary life—your sleeping, eating, going-to-work, and walking-around life—and place it before God as an offering. Embracing what God does for you is the best thing you can do for him" (Romans 12:1, MSG).

That's real worship. When Paul wrote that, it would have sounded completely radical. Why? Because offerings at that time would have been animal sacrifices. His readers had probably seen actual animal sacrifices. The Jews were still sacrificing animals at the time, and even some people of pagan religions performed animal sacrifices. People could picture the animal in their minds. They could see the knife slice its throat. They could see all the blood. And they could see the dead animal lying there on the altar as a gift to God or a god, depending on who was doing the sacrifice. The blood covered the sins of the people.

But Christians don't have to bleed and die to pay for sins. Our sins are covered by Jesus' blood. That's why Paul said we should offer our bodies as bloodless, *living* sacrifices. We should *give* our lives to God as volunteers and use our alive-again lives to serve Him—climb up on the altar and stay there by our own choice.

But what does that look like? How do we really *know* what God wants us to do? Two ways. (You'll find them both in Romans 12:2.) First, break out of the world's mold. Notice how the world around you lives, and don't get sucked into that like you're some kind of corporate-sponsored robot.

Second, let God make you new by changing your mind. Replace all your old ways of thinking with His new way of looking at things. It's kind of like trying to erase everything off a computer's hard drive and reinstalling new software. For us that means reading, studying, and memorizing His words from the Bible. Then, God promised, you'll know exactly what He wants you to do. That sounds easy, but it's not. It takes time, practice, discipline, and sacrifice—and even then we sometimes mess things up.

7. DESTINATION: HEAVEN

Ever take a long car trip with your family to the ocean or the mountains or Disney World? It can be grueling, can't it? You're hot, tired, hungry, grumpy—and that's just after the first hour and a half.

Remember that annoying question you and your siblings started asking about four hours before the trip was over? "Are we there yet?" Here's the point. Even if we live as Jesus' hands and feet, even if we become more and more like Christ, we're never going to be completely satisfied or happy in this life. There's nothing you can do, no decisions you can make, that will completely fill up that emptiness inside of you.

We do have God's Holy Spirit to comfort us and give us joy, peace, and love (see Galatians 5:22-23). That makes life worth living. That gives us power to live for our purpose to be Jesus' hands and feet. But this life can be hard and sometimes lonely.

Our real life is in heaven with Jesus; it's not here during this long, hot car trip. That's what all this is for. Heaven is where Jesus' path took Him, so naturally that's where His followers will end up, as stated in Colossians 3:1-4:

> *If then you were raised with Christ, seek those things which are above, where Christ is, sitting at the right hand of God. Set your mind on things above, not on things on the earth. For you died, and your life is hidden with Christ in God. When Christ who is our life appears, then you also will appear with Him in glory.*

BOOTS ON

Okay, this is it—decision time. Are you going to try to get comfortable here, or are you going to strap on your boots and start hiking after the One who died for you? Are you going to use your hands and feet to try to make your dreams come true, or are you going to use them to fulfill Jesus' mission?

A branch of the military used to have as its slogan "The toughest job you'll ever love." Following Jesus, living as His hands and feet, is much, much tougher. And you won't always love it. But you'll never find a path that's more worth your time, your commitment, and your life.

HANDS AND FEET IN ACTION

I stood with a death grip on the railing of the world's oldest active passenger ship. I waited patiently, knowing that at any second, breakfast was coming up and I would be feeding the fish of the South China Sea. At twenty-two years of age, I was seasick for the first time.

Just a couple of weeks earlier, I had flown from the States to Germany and then from Germany to the Philippines, where I joined a team of 320 missionaries — 320 amazing people from 35 different countries — who were ready and willing to know God and make Him known!

So this was it, the beginning of a two-year commitment. It was my first voyage, my first real taste of life out in the wild blue yonder. It was a simple two-day sail from Subic Bay, Philippines, to a small surf town called San Fernando City, Philippines.

On that first day, the water was unbelievably smooth. I remember thinking, If this is what ship life is going to be like, these two years will be heaven! *But I wasn't so fortunate. On the second day, the waves picked up and I stood teeth clenched, stomach turning, and knuckles as white as the pale moon. I thought for sure I was going to puke. Then, miraculously and for no apparent reason, I suddenly felt 100 percent better! I couldn't believe it. The seasickness passed, and I felt like a million dollars. As my death grip let up and my knuckles turned back to their normal flesh color, I was just about to head back inside. Then I thought to myself,* I might as well enjoy the fresh air while I'm out here.

I noticed a girl standing just forward of me who was also holding tight to the rail. This poor girl wasn't as fortunate as I. Then again, I wasn't so fortunate either. If you know anything about downward wind, you can imagine what happened. That's right—a good part of that girl's breakfast smacked me right in the face. I stood there, covered in vomit, thinking that my decision to join the ship for two long years was the biggest mistake of my life! But now I know that nothing could have been further from the truth.

My time onboard the M.V. Doulos *was unbelievably amazing. I saw Jesus do things through me that I could never do. I saw Jesus being the person through me that I could never be. Day after day, I would wake up in my seven-foot-by-seven-foot cabin, located under the waterline at the very bottom of the ship, and pray, "Father, I want You to know that, whether I feel like it or not, I'm totally available to You. Live Your life through me in a way that people know without a doubt that it's You doing the living and not Aaron Peterson." And that He did. Even though ship life is hard, even though normal life is hard, miracles happen when we're simply available to God.*

About two weeks into my two years, I found myself standing in front of twenty-five blank-faced, tattooed Filipino sailors, telling them that God wanted to have an intimate relationship with each of them.

The Doulos *had carried twenty of my shipmates and me to a week of firefighter training. Taking the course with us were thirty Filipino sailors, most in their forties and fifties. These men had spent a large portion of their lives sailing the world. When you hear the phrase "That person curses like a sailor," well, that's because most sailors are rough and tough and they curse — a lot.*

On the last day of our training, we decided to invite these thirty men to a small program we were performing. It wouldn't be glamorous, but we knew there was absolutely nothing else to do way out in the middle of the jungle.

To be completely honest, I was worried. I could imagine the guys getting bored and wandering back to their bunks. When the time came, about twenty-five of the men showed up. Some of us Doulos *guys sang some funny songs, some of us did a drama, and, mysteriously, I was nominated to give the gospel presentation and an invitation for the guys to accept Christ.*

I sat waiting through the program with sweaty palms, ignoring the mosquito that was ready to pop as he enjoyed a tasty evening meal on my arm. I was scared but also available to God. I wanted Jesus to speak to these guys.

When my turn came, I preached for a good three hours. Okay, not really. In fact, I didn't preach at all. I spoke for about ten minutes as simply and clearly as I possibly could, trusting that the words I spoke were not my own. Surprisingly, these Filipino sailors seemed to be hanging on every word I said. I closed by saying, "Guys, if you would like to experience an intimate relationship with the Creator of the world, I invite you to accept Jesus today. I'll lead you in asking Him to come into your life. As I speak, you speak after me. You can do it silently or you can do it out loud. Either way, do it with your heart knowing that you're speaking to a God who loves you very much."

As I prayed, I heard a sound that I'll never forget! A number of these hard sailors began to pray out loud and their voices harmonized together like the Brooklyn Tabernacle Choir. It was truly overwhelming, and it was all I could do to keep from crying right there in the middle of that life-changing prayer.

People all over this small planet we call Earth are hungry and desperate for something real. They're tired of empty religion! They're ready to accept Truth!

I could tell you about Pattaya, Thailand, where ten-year-old girls are forced into prostitution. I could tell you about Miri, Malaysia, where a thirty-five-year-old demon-possessed man has been locked in a tiny cage for the past four years of his life. I could tell you about village after village, town after town, city after city where materialism and meaningless attempts to grab on to happiness rob people from experiencing real life — real life, which comes only through the life of Jesus Christ.

Jesus gave His life for *us, to give His life* to *us, so He could live His life* through *us. He's looking for some radical Christians who will simply say, "I'm available!"*

—AARON, M.V. DOULOS, *2000-2002*

FIFTY WAYS TO BE JESUS' HANDS AND FEET IN YOUR NEIGHBORHOOD

1. Mow someone's lawn without asking for money.

2. Watch someone's kids while he or she goes shopping.

3. Hold a vacation Bible school in your backyard.

4. Go caroling at Christmas.

5. Organize a kid's parade on July 4.

6. Offer to pick up someone's groceries.

7. Take a meal to someone who's sick.

8. Buy a magazine subscription or box of cookies from neighbor kids during a school fund-raiser.

9. Visit neighbors who can't go out.

10. Pray for a different household on your block every day.

11. Help your neighbors shovel out after a big snow.

12. Help some kids set up a lemonade stand.

13. Offer to go jogging or roller-blading with a neighbor who wants to get in shape.

14. Invite a different neighbor to come to your church each month.

15. Ask if you can watch a neighbor kid's sporting event or play.

16. Volunteer to coach a neighborhood soccer team.

17. Host a block party.

18. Go door-to-door on your block asking your neighbors what you could do to help them.

19. Find the neighbor with the most kids and offer to help clean the house.

20. Offer a neighbor a ride.

21. Start a neighbors-only Bible study in your house.

22. Keep your home orderly so that it reflects well on the neighborhood.

23. Buy a card for neighbors who lose loved ones.

24. Offer to weed someone's flowerbed.

25. Hand out flyers offering to tutor kids in a subject you're good at.

26. Deliver Christmas cards with clear statements about who Jesus is to each house on the block.

27. Host a safe haunted house at Halloween.

28. Take a plate of cookies to new people in the neighborhood.

29. On a nice day, set up a free neighbors-only car wash.

30. Buy a funny encouragement card and leave it on a neighbor's door when you know he or she is having a bad day.

31. Hold a going-away party when a longtime neighbor is moving out of the neighborhood.

32. If you're in a rough neighborhood or one with lots of kids, organize a Neighborhood Watch group.

33. Publish a neighborhood newsletter with info about events and news about births, moves, and other positive happenings.

34. Make small talk at the mailbox.

35. Play catch with the kids in the front yard.

36. Send a congratulations card when someone gets a new car.

37. Refrain from saying anything bad about one neighbor to another.

38. Spend some time thanking God for each of your neighbors.

39. Ask a neighbor with a really nice lawn how he or she does that.

40. Offer to walk someone's dog once a week.

41. Don't pass up an opportunity to talk about your relationship with Jesus.

42. If you have a dog, scoop up everything!

43. Start a neighborhood book group.

44. When you hear the ice cream man, offer to buy someone a treat.

45. Go door-to-door handing out flowers on May Day.

46. Offer to host a neighborhood garage sale.

47. Treat everyone in the neighborhood with sexual purity.

48. Offer to dog-sit or house-sit when someone goes on vacation.

49. Host a spa day for your friends.

50. When people ask why you do all this stuff, be ready to tell them about Jesus.

FIFTY WAYS TO BE JESUS' HANDS AND FEET IN YOUR FAMILY

1. Take out the trash.

2. Obey your parents.

3. Give unconditional love to your siblings.

4. Pray for your mom to treat your dad the way God asked her to.

5. Walk the dog.

6. Look for opportunities to forgive.

7. Don't say too much when you're overly hungry.

8. Do the dishes when it's not your turn.

9. Thank your mom and dad for working so hard to earn money for the family.

10. Pray for your dad to treat your mom the way God told him to.

11. Come home on time or call to let your parents know where you are.

12. Treat your mom the way you'd want her to treat you if your roles were reversed.

13. Find one good thing to say about or to a sibling every day.

14. Laugh with your family.

15. Talk a little about what's going on in your life, even if it doesn't come naturally.

16. Ask God to give your parents wisdom about how to raise you and your siblings.

17. Set a Christlike example for the members of your family, even your parents (see 1 Timothy 4:12).

18. Offer to help clean the house when it's not your job.

19. Tell the cook what you enjoyed most about the meal.

20. Take time to laugh about some of your best family memories.

21. Turn off the TV when you recognize a good chance to talk about something meaningful.

22. Ask your parents about their relationships with God.

23. Ask your parents about their relationship with each other.

24. Don't leave the car on empty when you borrow it.

25. Ask your siblings if they see anything in your life that's keeping you from being more like Jesus.

26. Talk about your day at church together after it's over.

27. Write an encouraging note and leave it in a creative place where a friend or family member will find it.

28. Tape someone's favorite show so he or she doesn't miss it.

29. Go to other family members' performances or sporting events.

30. Organize a family prayer time, especially during a big event or difficult season of life.

31. Introduce your parents and siblings to your friends.

32. Learn to laugh at yourself.

33. Thank God for a different member of your family every day, and tell Him what's good about that person.

34. Make dinner or bring home a dessert for everyone.

35. Offer to exercise with a family member who'd like to get in shape.

36. Offer to help a sibling with studying or homework.

37. Ask God to help your parents spend the family's money wisely.

38. Look for reasons to compliment other family members on their appearance, actions, or attitudes.

39. Ask God to help any unsaved family members come to know Jesus as Savior.

40. When it's natural, don't be afraid to talk about your relationship with God.

41. When you fight, fight fair. Keep it about the issue and avoid getting too personal.

42. When you get angry, cool down before talking or acting.

43. Be aware when you're in a bad mood, and ask God to help you be patient and careful with your words.

44. Offer to drive people where they need to go.

45. Without attacking the other person, be honest when something's bothering you.

46. Offer to do a little more than is expected of you.

47. Look for ways to show your parents you respect them.

48. Don't lie. Ever.

49. Enjoy the fun times you have together.

50. Be ready to talk honestly about the difference Jesus has made in your life.

FIFTY WAYS TO BE JESUS' HANDS AND FEET AT YOUR SCHOOL

1. Eat lunch with someone who looks lonely.

2. Treat your teachers with respect.

3. If someone doesn't show up for a day or two, ask about it when he or she gets back.

4. Organize a study group for a big test.

5. Don't lie. Ever.

6. Learn to laugh at yourself.

7. Learn not to laugh at people who don't laugh at themselves.

8. Offer to spend extra time practicing with someone who is struggling with a sport.

9. If someone opens up a little, take time to listen.

10. Share your lunch.

11. Go to your friends' musical performances.

12. Offer rides.

13. Pray for your principal.

14. Take people seriously.

15. When it's natural, talk about Jesus.

16. Invite a friend to come to your youth group.

17. If someone is open to it, share music from Christian artists.

18. Don't cheat. Ever.

19. Start a student-led prayer group.

20. Go out for a sport or join a club with people you don't know very well.

21. Compliment people when they do something well.

22. Pray for the three people you like the least.

23. Ask a close Christian friend at school what in your life might get in the way of letting others see Jesus in you.

24. Challenge close Christian friends when they seem to be doing things that don't match up with what they say they believe.

25. Offer to lead a students-only Bible study.

26. Offer to disciple a Christian student who is two or three years younger than you.

27. Buy birthday cards for people who would least expect to get one from you.

28. Tell those on student government that you appreciate all the time they put into their jobs.

29. Out of respect for your teachers, don't sleep in class or skip without telling them why.

30. Smile at and make eye contact with people who don't seem to feel good about themselves.

31. Without being preachy, make sure your life is an example of sexual purity.

32. If someone asks what you believe about God, be ready to tell him or her about your faith in clear, simple words.

33. Laugh at other people's jokes when they're funny (unless they're at someone else's expense).

34. Talk respectfully about your parents.

35. Don't say anything bad or hurtful about another person, especially if you don't know for sure that it's true.

36. Say at least one encouraging thing to someone every day.

37. If someone expresses a strong belief in something that's not biblical, be ready to ask a couple of respectful but challenging questions.

38. Avoid saying God's or Jesus' name as a swear word.

39. Look for opportunities to forgive people who hurt you.

40. When you get angry, give yourself time to cool down before saying too much to or about the person who ticked you off.

41. Initiate conversations with especially shy people.

42. When having lunch with your friends, ask an unlikely person to join you and include him or her in your conversation.

43. To open up spiritual conversations, ask other people what they believe about God.

44. Do art projects on subjects that glorify God in a creative or interesting way.

45. Thank God for the people in your first period class.

46. Avoid being critical or judgmental of others' choices or beliefs, especially if they're not Christians.

47. Treat everyone the way you'd want to be treated.

48. Invite people over to your house (if it's okay with your parents).

49. If you're on a team, give your best effort as a way to respect your teammates.

50. When people ask why you're so different, be ready to tell them about Jesus.

ABOUT THE AUTHORS

AUDIO ADRENALINE has continued to build an ever-widening fan base over the years, with sales approaching three million units. The band has garnered four Grammy Award nominations and multiple Dove Awards. They have released a total of seventeen number-one songs, including fan favorite "Big House," which was named the CCM Song of the Decade for the 1990s. With their first book, *Dirty Faith*, and their latest album, *Worldwide*, Audio Adrenaline continues to communicate their message of missions and outreach to thousands of devoted fans.

MARK MATLOCK is the founder of WisdomWorks Ministries and creator of PlanetWisdom.com, an incredible Internet resource for teens, parents, and youth pastors. Mark also hosts the nationally syndicated radio program *WisdomWorks*. An ordained minister, he teaches at PlanetWisdom conferences for teens and Generation Hope seminars for parents. Mark is the author of several books and has conducted nationwide studies with Barna Research on teens, evangelism, and the supernatural. Mark and his wife, Jade, reside with their two children, Dax and Skye, in Irving, Texas.

ABOUT MISSION YEAR

Mission Year is a dynamic movement of believers dedicated to building the kingdom of God through sacrificial service. Every day our team members put their faith into action in inner-city neighborhoods across the nation, providing a powerful combination of community service and Christian love. They tutor, build, nurture, repair, encourage, assist, organize, teach, learn from, listen to, and pray with all kinds of people, all in the name of Jesus. To find out more, go to www.missionyear.org.

No games, no masks—God accepts us as we are.

Posers, Fakers, & Wannabes
Unmasking the Real You
Brennan Manning and Jim Hancock
1-57683-465-4

God isn't fooled by the games we play, the masks we wear. And as much as we try, we'll never fake our way into his affection.

The best part is: the Father already knows and accepts us exactly as we are. He knows how we think and act; He knows our dreams and fears. Brennan and Jim explain how God's total acceptance of us sets us free to be who we really are.

1-800-366-7788
www.th1nkbooks.com
THINK

Get the Bible off your shelf and into your heart.

Memorize This: TMS 3.0
1-57683-457-3

Why memorize anything? Laptops, cell phones, PDAs do all the memorizing for you, right? Well, not really. When you need something RIGHT NOW, it needs to be stored in your heart.

That's how God's Word should be — so when something happens, it's right there. After all, how did Jesus handle temptation? He quoted God's Word in its face. A specialized version of NavPress's successful *Topical Memory System*, this book will help you deal with whatever life throws at you — if the words are in your heart, and not just in your machines.

1-800-366-7788
www.th1nkbooks.com

Because they don't offer Talking to God 101.
(Even though they should.)

pray
Tony Jones
1-57683-452-2

Do you ever feel a little stumped about prayer—like you keep saying the same things over and over again? Maybe you don't know how to get started.

With this book, you'll learn by the solid example of those who have gone before us. The prayers of these men and women—the prophets, the apostles, the early and modern church, and even Jesus Himself—can help us pray more effectively. Author Tony Jones highlights the important features of these powerful prayers—so you can enjoy talking to God as much as they did.

1-800-366-7788
www.th1nkbooks.com

THINK

Practice your faith. Every day.

Read, Think, Pray, Live
A guide to reading the Bible in a new way
Tony Jones
1-57683-453-0

If you want to know Jesus and what He's all about, try doing these four: read, think, pray, live. It's how your faith can grow. *Lectio divina*, or sacred reading, is a time-tested method used by believers to experience God in a personal and real way.

Tailored for students, this book teaches you how to engage your faith. Learning from a method of contemplative study that has worked for hundreds of years, you'll find yourself challenged and encouraged to get to know God in brand-new ways.

1-800-366-7788
www.th1nkbooks.com
TH1NK

Knowing God isn't just a walk—it's a chase.

The Chase
Pursuing Holiness in Your Everyday Life
Jerry Bridges
1-57683-468-9

The Bible calls us to be holy. Is that even possible? There must have been some glitch in the translation, right?

That depends on your definition of holy. If by it you mean "always perfect, never making a mistake," you're right—that's impossible. But if by holy you mean "wanting and doing the right things," that can be done with the aid of the Holy Spirit.

Taken from the NavPress classic *The Pursuit of Holiness*, this book shows students how "running as to get the prize" isn't just possible, it's what life is all about.

1-800-366-7788
www.th1nkbooks.com
THINK

What if He were born in Bethlehem . . . Pennsylvania?

!HERO Comics and Graphic Novel

Comic 1: 1-57683-504-9
Comic 2: 1-57683-501-4
Comic 3: 1-57683-502-2
Comic 4: 1-57683-503-0
*Graphic Novel: 1-57683-500-6

*Includes comics 1-4 plus the previously unreleased comic 5

Follow the !HERO action up close and personal! Read as
Special Agent Alex Hunter strives to discover the story
behind a mysterious miracle-worker from Bethlehem,
Pennsylvania, whose very presence is changing the world.

In a series of five action-packed episodes, best-selling
author Stephen R. Lawhead, collaborating with author
and penciler Ross Lawhead, incites the imagination to
wonder: What if He were born today? Collect all four
comics, then pick up the graphic novel to get issue five!

Check out www.herouniverse.com for more information.

1-800-366-7788
www.th1nkbooks.com

The Message Remix
Eugene H. Peterson
Hardback
1-57683-434-4
Bonded Alligator Leather
1-57683-450-6

God's Word was meant to be read and understood. It was first written in the language of the people — of fishermen, shopkeepers, and carpenters. *The Message Remix* gets back to that feel. Plus the new verse-numbered paragraphs make it easier to study.

Promises. Promises. Promises.
Eugene H. Peterson
1-57683-466-2

Everybody's making promises these days.
But who's really true to their word?

God is. Take a look at His promises — promises of a real life and a future. See how knowing them can help you trust God even more.

The Message:
The Gospel of John
in Contemporary Language
Eugene H. Peterson
1-57683-432-8

Read what John witnessed as he walked alongside Jesus. Then help others find hope and a new way of life — better and more real than they've ever dreamed of experiencing. Share it with everyone you know!